THRIVING
IN CONFLICT

THRIVING
IN CONFLICT

HOW TO BUILD A ROBUST CULTURE OF FEEDBACK

DOUG JOHNSTON

MOUNTAIN ARBOR
PRESS

Mountain Arbor
Press
Alpharetta, GA

ISBN: 978-1-63183-664-0 - Paperback
eISBN: 978-1-63183-665-7 - ePub
eISBN: 978-1-63183-666-4 - Mobi

Library of Congress Control Number: 2019915588

Printed in the United States of America   1 0 0 3 1 9

♾ This paper meets the requirements of ANSI/NISO Z39.48-1992 (Permanence of Paper)

To Francine, Emily, and David, my reason for all I do.

At the end of the day, we all have the responsibility to engineer the necessary conversations to realize impactful results.

Contents

Introduction

If you have picked up this book, you might be hoping it will provide you with everything you need to get back at that coworker who is a royal pain in the butt. Or you might hope it will help you quell all workplace conflicts so everyone can live in peaceful harmony.

I am sorry to disappoint you. But I think you will find that this book will provide you with ideas and tools to deal with conflict when it happens. To deal with it in new ways and to create better results in our work and in our lives. It's like Gandhi said: "Honest disagreement is often a good sign of progress." If we can work with the inevitable conflicts we are going to experience, maybe we can accomplish great things.

Human relations are imperfect by nature; they are messy and at times fraught with peril. When we can embrace that, we have found opportunity. It is through that dysfunction that we can come to a higher understanding and better relationships.

I know I come into the workplace with my own set of baggage. Sometimes that gets in the way of my work with other people. There might be more than one occasion where my name was mentioned in therapy, and it wasn't when my therapist called me back to schedule my own appointment. I will never be perfect, never, and that is an absolute truth. So if I bring in my own dysfunction, shouldn't I be a little more tolerant of the dysfunction others may bring? And if that's true, shouldn't we make it our mission to work through these types of challenges as teams?

Having written this book, I may be suggesting that I am an expert at dealing with conflict. I am not. I don't know anyone who is. This is a lifelong struggle for me, as I think it is for everyone, and I probably fail as much as I succeed. Maybe even more. But if I were playing baseball, I would be happy if I could bat anywhere near 500. Our goal should not be perfection, but taking that risk of stepping up to the plate, gripping our bat, looking down the pipe that's hurling an object at you, sometimes at lethal speed, and swinging as best we can. Yes, we are going to miss, but when we connect, we can send the ball hurling over the fence.

Underlying the premise of this book is the fact that the universal tool we all have in our bag is our ability to engage in conversation. There is an old business axiom that says "Cash is king." But I think that misses an important element of business. So I modified that quote to: "Cash is king, but culture trumps all." Culture represents our ability to continue to generate cash. We have all seen organizations that are roadkill because they tried to merge failing cultures or the combined cultures didn't mesh. So what is culture? I believe it is nothing more than what we talk about and how we talk about it. That's why I think conversation is the universal tool that is central to everything.

If you buy into that, I hope this book does two things for you. First, I hope it gives you some different ways to think about the conversations you have. To see them as the lifeblood of our organizations and, quite honestly, our lives. If we change how we think about conversation, we can then change the shape of those conversations, the shape of our companies, and the quality of our results.

The second gift I hope this book provides is tools you can apply in the workplace. Just as we pick up relationships throughout our lives, so too do we collect tools. The lineman who restores power after big storms has bags full of tools, and even whole truckloads. So we too gather tools to help us do our jobs. That's why I have tried to provide simple tools you can apply in the workplace. Put them in your bag with your other tools and find opportunities to try them out.

I have not tried to create rote processes or systems for having conversations. There are far too many variables and situations we need to respond to. Instead, you will find frameworks. By that I mean a frame through which to look at a conversation, a frame of mind to use when considering conversations, a way to frame conversations, and a frame in which to have those conversations.

You will notice that each section is delineated by an infinity loop (∞). To me, this represents the essence of the feedback loops we need to create in the workplace. There is no beginning, and no end. It represents the importance of continuously collecting and adjusting to the environment around us. It also shows that our conversations are loops as well. The end of one conversation can lead naturally into the beginning of the next.

This is my second book, the first being *Exponential Leadership*. This book is not a sequel, and there is no need to read these books in any particular order. However, both books are written as stories. Why? Because I like stories. I have enjoyed reading both business and history, fiction and nonfiction. The one thing I've found that makes a book memorable is when it tells a compelling story. I often say that I may not remember the point, but I will surely remember a good story. I also find stories help guide us and imprint on our experiences in different ways. We are by nature storytellers, and we use these stories to teach and learn.

Even though the books are not directly related, I did bring back one character from the first book: our protagonist, Carolyn. People said they missed her after they finished the last book, so she is back in this book. Otherwise, the setting, context, and other characters are all new. Like I said, you don't need to have read the first book to get this one.

In the end, I hope I can entertain you and share some stories and tools to help you in your life. I hope you can sit back, read this book, and let the story wash over you to see how it moves you. Enjoy.

Chapter 1

Soul-Sucking Conflict

I feel like I've just finished another brutal boxing match: battered, bloodied, and bruised. That seems to be the general trend since I took this job a month ago. Every day ends with me collapsing into my favorite leather chair, feet up, eating whatever I can scrounge from the fridge or cupboard. And my cupboard's always envious of Mother Hubbard's famous pantry. Tonight it's crackers, peanut butter, and jelly.

The TV is on, but it's washing over me; I'm absorbing nothing. It's just background noise while I sort through the day. At the end of these days, I don't have the energy to move or to think. I'm just biding my time until I crash for the night hoping I get some sleep so I can start the same routine tomorrow.

I knew this job would require long hours, and I told myself I was ready for it. Why wouldn't I be? I worked long hours at my previous job. But each day is draining me, and I can't quite figure out what it is that's sapping me dry like a dewdrop under the rising desert sun. This is a different kind of exhaustion. It's not the sleep deprivation—I'm used to that—it's a deeper deprivation. It's like someone stuck a straw in my chest and is sucking the lifeblood from me.

I took this job to move back home to the Midwest to be closer to family. For the past ten years I lived on the West Coast working for one of those Silicon Valley success stories. I cut my teeth building customer support and enjoyed working for a fast-growth company that excelled as a leader in its field.

After two acquisitions, it was time for something new. I missed my family, and my previous job hadn't allowed me to build any kind of social network outside of those I worked with. Being closer to home and to family became of increasing importance to me, especially since I wanted to watch my sister's two young children grow up.

Some think the fast pace of Silicon Valley might be draining. It isn't. Of course, we were always resource constrained, chasing cash, pioneering new markets, and launching new products. There was an adrenaline high in that type of environment that kept you charged. My friend compared it to her job as an emergency room doctor. There is a high that comes from the rush of triage and the addiction it can create. I could relate.

Yet I never remember feeling this drained in my previous job. In this job, there is a difference, but I can't put my finger on it.

My current job is very similar to my previous job; customer support sits in the crosshairs between sales, operations, and engineering. Every day there is something happening, just like my previous job. Customer issues arise, sales needs help with a special customer request, operations comes rushing in with some urgent demand, and engineering is trying to make sure we don't rush so fast that we create problems down the road.

It all rings with the same set of challenges as my previous role. That job had the same triage feel my friend described, and so does this one.

I understand that this type of work isn't for everyone. I've seen plenty of managers put their foot down to stop the merry-go-round and get off the ride. For me, it is a thrill, and I remember looking forward to showing up every day.

There's a satisfaction in being able to get all the pieces working together, in revealing the unknown and seeing things get done. My previous job felt like all the gears were turning together. Customer support might have been the little gear in some people's minds, but like any gear system, the little gear turns fast and furious to make the bigger gears turn. It's not that the previous company was perfect. There were times when the gears came unhinged, overheated, or got stuck, but the team seemed to come together to get things realigned and turning again.

In this job, it feels like at any given moment one gear is turning against another. There is no meshing, no alignment. Because we are a sales-driving company, it seems like sales requests go to the front of the line, sometimes at the expense of the other functions. Engineering seems to be pushing in the clutch whenever we start to hum along, bringing things to a virtual standstill. Operations seems to be gun shy. They don't want to ship anything if there is any risk. It's an admirable trait unless it creates inertia, which it is doing.

Don't get me started on finance. They just want the numbers put in their spreadsheets. And boy, are there spreadsheets. I have a full-time person just populating data. I am not sure anyone even looks at the numbers or uses them to run the business.

Tomorrow is the weekly review meeting. All parties will be in the room, and when I say all parties, I mean all parties. I don't know who creates the invite list, but it seems like everyone gets handed a personalized invitation as they walk through the door that day. I've only been at the company for a month, so I have only attended four of these meetings. Each is pandemonium. Although it's an unfocused free-for-all, there is one common thread: no one seems to be in charge.

I need to get some sleep tonight so I have the strength to get through my fourth assault—I mean "review meeting"—tomorrow.

The weekly review meeting starts at 1:00 p.m. sharp every Thursday and ends promptly at 5:00 p.m. Actually, that isn't true; some see the one o'clock start time as a guideline. I've yet to see a meeting start anywhere near one o'clock. People straggle in and the meeting starts when there is a critical mass or someone tosses a topic on the table that can be addressed by someone else in the meeting.

I've seen people arrive for this meeting as late at four, causing a complete reboot of everything. The meetings never end at five; they only end through attrition—when enough people have left or people are too exhausted to carry on.

You can see some people carrying wounded soldiers out of the conference room. Others are left wounded on the conference room floor. Anyone lucky enough to leave under his or her own power crawls back to a foxhole and hunkers down for another week.

Today's meeting starts like the other four: someone lobs a hand grenade into the middle of the room and everyone dives for cover. It starts with statement like "Who did (something that created a problem)?" or "What happened to (some order or complaint)?" After that, the meeting devolves into mayhem. Hand grenades, bombshells, and mortars start flying.

The group jumps from one topic to the next, and although connected in some way, there is never clear closure to any given topic. Today we start with a special customer request. That leads to a full-on assault of IT for the system that doesn't support special requests. Sales jumps up on the pulpit, preaching about the importance of meeting the demands of an ever-changing market.

There are those you always hear from. They have something to say regardless of whether the topic relates to them. Conversely, there are some who just sit there quietly, saying nothing. Afterward, you aren't even sure they were in the meeting. It's like they have their own stealth technology that keeps anyone from taking a shot at them. Some just work on their laptops, taking up space but not adding anything. There are others who are clearly suffering from some form of PTSD.

There are things that get done in these meetings, but the cost in human lives—okay, more like human souls—is fairly significant. The company has probably been able to get by on this kind of brute force for years, but in the war of attrition, we will lose in the long term.

I am only half listening after a few hours of today's meeting. I am thinking about the conversation I had with the company president when I was first hired. She told me she needed someone to be a change agent in how we handle things from the time of an order to the time a customer is successfully using the product. After all, that is what I had done previously. I know she was sincere in her gesture, and I was eager to leave my own imprint on the company. Plus, I was excited to work in a company led by a strong female executive.

I awake from my little respite of a daydream that came upon me in the dwindling hours of our meeting. It's getting late in the day; the sun is already setting outside the conference room window. It's that mid-December hibernation period, when everyone in this part of the country is sun deprived. I haven't been at the company long enough to exert myself, but with the last gasp of energy before full twilight I decide to speak up.

When there is a small lull in the action, I hear these words come out of my mouth before I can pull them back in: "Can I ask a question? Is this working for you all?"

The group stops dead in its tracks, and I can't tell what emotions I just evoked from each person. Clearly the reaction is mixed. I can't put the toothpaste back in the tube now.

Peter, the head of sales, is the first to speak. "What do you mean, Angela?"

I take his question as a genuine query. "This is only the fourth time I've been in this review meeting, and I'm just wondering if this is working for everyone."

Clearly I hit a chord, because a rather raucous conversation ensues. I just watch to see where this will go, but it is clear this meeting isn't working for everyone, if anyone at all. After enough discussion, Peter turns back to me and says, "Well, you opened a can of tuna fish. What do you think about what you heard?" Peter has a fun way of using these types of metaphors with a jovial delivery.

"It sounds to me like the group doesn't really think this meeting is working for them."

Joanne from operations jumps in: "Well, what kind of suggestions do you have to bring to us from the Wild West?" Her question is more of a challenge than a question. Joanne has a sharp edge to her, and I don't think she really cares for me. I am the outsider, and she has been at the company for a long time. All of that aside, she is very good at her job, just hard to get along with.

Peter jumps in. "Now Joanne, let's not take out the new person—" he smiles in a teasing way—"quite so early in her tenure here." You can see why Peter is in sales; he's a charmer. But I also know that by saving me, at some point he will be showing up at my doorstep to collect on that little favor.

I don't take the bait right away, I just let the group continue. Once the conversation settles, I offer a couple of thoughts. "Maybe we need one person to lead the meeting, and we could have a little more focus and trim the attendees."

Heads nod, and it seems that made sense. I let it hang in the air because I am still new enough I don't want to overstep the boundaries of my honeymoon. Peter smiles at me. "Well, I think we just found our meeting leader."

Ouch, I didn't see that coming. I don't want that responsibility. I start to protest that I haven't been at the company long enough and I'm not sure I am the right person. I also know that if I take responsibility for this meeting, I become the "wring-able neck" when something goes badly.

Peter, the consummate salesperson, does a solid job convincing the group why it should be me. He explains that I am new to the company and have new ideas, while everyone else has been here too long and is too close to it. He adds that my previous company is seen as very successful, and we can learn from them. Lastly, customer service sits at the center of everything. Bam, Peter closes his deal.

By the time he's done, I am anointed leader of the weekly review meeting, everyone has left the room, and I'm sitting there wondering what the hell just happened. That goes to show, be careful when you speak up.

I have no idea how long I've been sitting there, or what time it is when I hear the sound of wheels coming down the hallway. It's the familiar sound of the cleaning cart; someone is going through the building cleaning up the ravages of the day. I don't think the ravages of this meeting can be tidied up.

The cleaning person comes in with a little more energy than I feel at the moment. She bounces in, ponytail poking through the back of her baseball hat, bobbing back and forth. She is middle aged and whistling lightly, barely audible until she is right near you.

She smiles and I smile back. I say thank-you as she takes away the wastepaper basket from the conference room. When she returns, I ask her name—Carolyn, she replies—and I offer mine. She reminds me of my sister, someone I have trusted my entire life. Which is why I feel comfortable enough to engage her in conversation.

I ask, "How long have you worked here?" to which she says, "I actually don't work here. My company provides the facility services for your company and this building." Although she doesn't say it directly, I surmise from her comment that she actually owns the company.

I ask her a bold question, not knowing what to expect or even why I would ask her. "What do you make of this place?"

She smiles. "What do you mean?"

"I've only been here a few weeks, and it seems all the right pieces are in place, but they don't mesh together. I can't quite make heads or tails of it. On top of that, I spoke up in today's meeting and now have responsibility for this weekly review meeting with not a clue where to begin. It feels like everyone is at odds with each other over every little thing."

After a bit of my rambling, she says, "Conflict can be very challenging."

That's the word that has been floating in the ether, but I have yet to say it: Conflict. "This place is loaded with conflicts," I continue. "It is in the air and permeates everything." Conflict is the straw that has been stuck in my side sucking the soul out of me. It has probably been doing the same to everyone else. "That's what I need to do, get rid of the conflicts. Crap, how do I do that?"

Carolyn says, "Who says you need to get rid of it?"

My startled gaze tells her I don't have a clue what she means. She continues: "Conflict is everywhere, right?" She looks to me to acknowledge.

I respond tentatively, "Yes."

"Think about it—not just here, conflict is everywhere. Have you ever been somewhere there isn't conflict?"

"Well no, but why is it different here? Sure, I've been around conflict, but it never felt like the soul was being sucked out of me like it has in the past few weeks."

"Conflict is soul sucking when we don't deal with it. But on the flip side, conflict can also propel us forward, can't it?" she asks, without really looking for an answer.

CONFLICT CAN BE SOUL SUCKING WHEN WE DON'T DEAL WITH IT, OR IT CAN PROPEL US FORWARD.

"Have you ever had conflict in a way that really helped the organization? Where it moved things forward, and it didn't suck the energy out of everyone?" I share with her the experience in my previous job, and it occurs to me that we were always in conflict, but we used it like a springboard to move forward. I start thinking to myself, *What's the difference?*

Carolyn starts to get up and says, "It seems to me you might want to rethink how you define conflict. That would be a good place to start." She bounces out of the room, bidding me good evening. I feel a little lightened for about a minute. Then I realize, *What am I supposed to do with that, and how is it going to help me get this meeting working?*

Carolyn's voice echoes down the hallway as she recedes. "Remember, redefine conflict."

The next day I arrive at my office before the sun rises. A usual pattern for me, but easier to do this time of year during the dark days of winter. I am the first one in this morning, and my mind is still reeling from yesterday—first from the chaos of the weekly review meeting that left me anointed its new leader, but secondly from the conversation with Carolyn where she challenged me to "redefine conflict." Obviously she sees a connection between these two things. I am not so sure.

Still, I go to my whiteboard and write:

CONFLICT

I sit back in my chair and look at what I wrote, hoping some great insight would be divined from looking at the word.

Nothing.

I go to my computer to look up the definition of conflict. I get a few different descriptions.

> *A serious disagreement or argument, typically a protracted one.*
>
> *Be incompatible or at variance; clash.*
>
> *Competitive or opposing action of incompatibles: antagonistic state or action (as of divergent ideas, interests, or persons) a conflict of principles.*
>
> *Mental struggle resulting from incompatible or opposing needs, drives, wishes, or external or internal demands.*
>
> *The opposition of persons or forces that gives rise to the dramatic action in a drama or fiction.*

Well, that's a bit disheartening. No wonder I've always wanted to avoid conflict. Words like argument, clash, incompatible, struggle, and opposition are all fairly inflammatory. I'm sure everyone feels this way, except maybe Joanne, our operations lead, who seems to like creating conflict.

Just then, my phone rings and startles me out of my thoughts. It's a welcome call from my friend Carl, who worked with me at my previous company.

As we greet each other, I look at my clock and realize it's early in my time zone, even earlier for him on the West Coast. I ask him what he is doing up so early.

"Actually, I am in your town for some vendor visits. I have a free lunch, any chance I can take you out for a bite?"

"Sure!" It would be great to see a friendly face. Carl was probably one of my closest confidants at my last company. We navigated many a storm in our work journey. Our groups were naturally at odds with each other, but I never felt we were in . . .

And I look up at the word scrawled on my whiteboard: *Conflict.* Maybe Carl can offer some thoughts.

We make arrangements to meet at a pub around the corner and bid farewell until our lunch meeting.

The morning flies by as usual. I am getting the typical barrage of urgent requests. Between interruptions, I am making a list of things that need to be addressed to improve our weekly review meeting. Some items are pretty straightforward. I am making notes in my journal as they occur to me:

Start on time. It is so disruptive when people show up late. We have to rewind to rehash items already covered, and it sends a message to the other people in the meeting that their time is not as important. We will need to come up with a way to deal with situations where someone gets detained and can't get to the meeting on time. For example, they can have an alternate ready to jump in for them, or they can have someone in the meeting bring them up to speed after or during a break. Nevertheless, the expectation is to start on time. I vow not to punish the compliant who show up on schedule.

End on time. Just like it is disrespectful to people to start late, so too is it disrespectful to consistently run over. Either set the end time later so people can plan accordingly, or end on time and take remaining topics offline. I think if we just keep to an organized agenda and start on time, this will be much easier.

Limit attendees. There are key people who need to be in the room to make decisions. Those are the people who need to be at the table. And that doesn't mean those with the highest seniority. Many of the decisions we need to make are from those on the front line who are in contact with customers and doing the work. I am sure many of the attendees who are invited to the meeting, on the outside chance they get asked a question, would relish the opportunity to go back to their workspace and get real work done. We can recommend that people make sure they are available during the meeting if we need to dial them in or have them join us. The key to the attendees is "decisions." It seems the more people who attend, the less the likelihood someone will make a decision. It's like when you have a group of adults watching children. The amount of adult supervision is disproportionate to the number of adults in attendance.

Organize the agenda. I don't like the term agenda; it can be too constraining. Plus, I've seen too many meetings with structured agendas that don't get anything accomplished. I look above and notice the word "decisions" and realize we need to organize around decisions. So instead of "agenda," I decide we should call it "decision points." Just as the attendees need to be those who make decisions, the agenda needs to reflect the decisions we need to make.

I start to list the key decisions we need to make and organize them by topic. For example, "orders" is a topic, and it includes expedited order requests, prioritizing backlog, and forecast for orders produced in the next week. I have underlined "key decisions for each."

CAN CONFLICT LEAD TO BETTER DECISIONS?

These all seem like they will help, but I don't get a feeling they will ultimately solve the soul-sucking force in our company's air. I look up at the word Conflict and realize that although this might reduce some of the conflicts, it doesn't get to the heart of the issue. Then I make a note that by focusing on decisions, we might be teasing out the conflicts we need to address.

I don't feel I've made any progress on redefining conflict, and although I have some thoughts for the Thursday review meeting, I feel like I am only putting a box around the work, but not really addressing *how* we work together.

The proverbial lunch bell rings, and I am off to meet up with Carl.

Lunch is spent in a corner booth of a dark Irish pub frequented by the downtown lunch crowd. It's a busy Friday, but our spot gives us some privacy, and we don't have to shout over the crowd. It is good to catch up. Carl fills me in on the latest at my former company and some of the changes since the latest acquisition. He ended up with a promotion and now runs a larger team that is consolidated with the others from the acquiring company.

He describes the challenges forthwith, but he seems to have a handle on them. After he has exhausted all the updates on the business and our former colleagues, he pivots to ask about me. He starts with, "So are you happy?" I get the sense he is testing me and might even have been sent on a mission to get me to come back. I appreciated the company's efforts to keep me when I resigned. God knows I would find great comfort in being back in an environment that's more functional than this.

I tell him I'm happy to be back near family, and I share the joys of getting to see my niece and nephew regularly. I share with him my trials from the past few weeks, and he laughs with me as we realize how some things are funny because they're true. I share with him how one of my programmers showed up in a T-shirt that said, "I don't always test my code, but when I do, it is in production."

I stopped by his desk later that day and asked him about his shirt in a jovial way. I hoped and prayed that he tested his code in the test environment, not live in production. Usually I would take that type of thing as a joke, but we had two system crashes in two weeks and no explanations. He assured me it was only a joke, but smiled a devilish smile that left me wondering. Carl laughs, but the type of laugh a parent has when they watch their kids struggle with their own children.

I share with him the weekly review meeting and how I got sucked into running it. He agrees with Peter that I am probably the best person for the job, for all the same reasons. I appreciate his vote of confidence, but it doesn't resolve my uneasiness.

I explain the notes I made this morning about the meeting structure. They include many of the same things we did at our previous company: decision makers in the room, keeping the attendees list small, start and end times, people on call when needed, etc. He liked the direction and made some suggestions.

Then I start to explain my conversation with Carolyn, trying to define conflict and the undercurrent that permeates many of the conversations at the company. Carl and I discuss how he and I were often in conflict, but I explain that it had a different feel to it. Sure, there were times we were at odds over things like priorities, who got what resources, and the cause of problems we encountered. But we got through them together, even when we agreed to disagree. And it wasn't just the two of us; that was the general experience with most people you worked with at my previous employer.

I explain how the dictionary definition of conflict didn't fit, and actually made me more uncomfortable. Carl takes my challenge and starts poking at the concept of conflict. We go back and forth looking at various situations from our previous experiences working together. There comes a theme from our examples, like "Someone wanted this and got that," "We need this by a certain date and got it on another date," "I expected someone to show up at one time and they showed up at another," and even situations like Joanne, where someone's communication style can be caustic. The list goes on.

Carl pulls out a three-by-five card from a folio he always has handy and writes down one word—GAP—and proceeds to explain that all situations we are discussing represent one thing: a gap. It makes sense; conflict is a gap. We smile at our brilliance and spend the rest of the lunch bantering about our mutual disdain for the local university football team. We are both Big Blue fans, even though neither of us went there.

HOW CAN WE SEE THE GAP WE EXPERIENCE IN CONFLICT?

I keep waiting for Carl to drop a topical nudge back to the direction of my previous employer, but it doesn't come. I don't think it's because he doesn't want me there; I think he respects this move as something I need to do, and also the need for family at this point in my life. He lets me pick up the tab for lunch as payment for coming up with the word "gap." It is a cheap investment, as I feel a little better and have some ideas.

We say our goodbyes at the pub and agree to stay in touch. I turn down the street to walk back toward my office. For a moment, I feel my step has lightened, but each step forward seems to weigh me down again. A gap. *So what*, I think. It is a thought, but far from a complete thought.

When I get back to my office, I write our word up on the whiteboard after the word Conflict so that now it says:

CONFLICT: A GAP.

Throughout the afternoon, between calls and interruptions, I keep looking up at the whiteboard hoping something will jump out at me. I am reflecting on the conversation with Carl and ask myself, *What is the gap?* Thinking about all the examples we discussed, it comes to me that the gap is between expectation and experience. When we are in conflict, it is because something happens and we expect one thing, but we get something else. I go to the whiteboard and I erase the period and continue the sentence.

CONFLICT: A GAP BETWEEN WHAT WE <u>EXPECT</u> AND WHAT WE <u>EXPERIENCE</u>.

I capitalize and underline the key words, feeling satisfied with my little flash of brilliance.

The bustle of the day has diminished and the early setting sun is casting shadows into my office. It's Friday, and I declare victory for the day and the week. I grab my coat and head out to meet some old friends for happy hour. The privileges of being home.

Saturday morning finds me back at my desk enjoying my favorite foo-foo frappuccino latte, or whatever they call the coffee of the day at the corner bistro. I need to get caught up on things, and I still don't have a plan for Thursday's meeting. I glance up at my writing on the whiteboard and still feel something missing: a big why. Why do I care, why would anyone else care if there is a gap? People only care if they get their way.

As I am doing these mental gymnastics, I hear the cleaning-cart wheels coming down the hall, and I'm hopeful it's Carolyn. She comes bouncing into my office like a hyperactive squirrel all jacked up on caffeine. This woman is a force of nature. She seems shocked to see me and says hello and asks how things are going. I am equally shocked she is working on a Saturday.

I ask her if she has a minute as I gesture toward one of the extra chairs in my office. I wheel my chair over to the small discussion table I use when I have visitors.

I ask her what brings her in on a Saturday. She explains that Saturday is what they call a "special service day." It is a time when they can tidy up and service the office better than weekdays, when people might be working late. I had wondered who did that. There are always nice touches to the office, like seasonal accents, as well as stocked mini-fridges and snack dishes. It's what her business does to leave little extra touches to make her customers happy and keep the office a little more inviting.

I point her toward the whiteboard to show her my homework. She smiles and nods with approval. "I like how you are using something as simple as a gap to define conflict." Then she adds, "I notice a little furrow on your brow. Something still puzzling you?"

"Yeah, it seems like something is missing. The word 'why' keeps coming to my mind. Like 'Why would anyone care about conflict?' Either they will avoid it or seek the easiest path to get what they want, regardless of others."

She agrees. "That does seem like a legitimate concern. Tell me more about your last company. You said it wasn't the same. What was the difference?"

I have to pause to really think about it. My mind goes to Carl and how we worked together at the previous company. "Carl and I were always in conflict because our jobs put us in that position. For example, he would need resources, and I had to constantly evaluate whether it was possible. Sometimes the answer was yes, other times it was no."

"How did you handle it when you said no?"

"What impressed me about Carl is that he really took the time to understand and listen. But he also had a way of sharing his thoughts that helped me understand his perspective. On many occasions, because we were listening to each other, we actually came up with creative ideas to solve challenges that neither of us would have ever conceived."

> **HOW CAN WE HAVE THE TIME AND PATIENCE TO LISTEN AND UNDERSTAND OTHERS' PERSPECTIVES WHEN IN CONFLICT?**

"And here?" Carolyn asks with a pregnant pause.

"In this company, it seems like everyone is myopic in their view. They don't try to understand; they focus only on what they want or need. They don't work together, and many times, like I mentioned the other day, they are working at odds with others."

Carolyn looks toward the ceiling with a thoughtful glance and then brings her gaze back to me. "I heard you use the word 'understand' several times. Does that fit anywhere in your definition?"

I move toward the whiteboard and grab a marker, with no idea yet as to what I'm going to write. I erase the period again at the end of what I had written previously. After a minute or two, I extend my definition a little further. It now says:

CONFLICT: A GAP BETWEEN WHAT WE <u>EXPECT</u> AND WHAT WE <u>EXPERIENCE</u> THAT LEADS TO DEEPER <u>UNDERSTANDING</u>.

That helps, but I'm still not satisfied. A piece is still missing. Carolyn lets me continue to ponder as I stare at the whiteboard. It still doesn't seem like it fully addresses the "why." After a long silence, it hits me like a lightning bolt. "Carl and I accomplished great things together. If we want conflict to propel us forward, it has to have something at stake, a result we need to accomplish." I erase the period again and finish the definition:

CONFLICT: A GAP BETWEEN WHAT WE <u>EXPECT</u> AND WHAT WE <u>EXPERIENCE</u> THAT LEADS TO DEEPER <u>UNDERSTANDING</u> AND BETTER <u>RESULTS</u>.

Carolyn compliments this piece of work and I thank her. "I can't thank you enough, I couldn't have done it without you."

As she gathers herself to finish her rounds, she humbly says, "I am honored to watch how you think this through. Thank you for including me."

Off she goes, and I sit back in the chair with a small smile of satisfaction. I sit forward, grab my phone, and type in the completed definition in a text message and hit send. No explanation, just the definition. I had to share it with someone. A few minutes later, I get one of those emoji responses. Five thumbs up in a row. I appreciate Carl's affirmation.

I keep looking up at the definition occasionally as I sort through the rubble of emails, authorizations, and audit results. I spend a few more hours in the office, but still have some uncertainty about how this definition relates to the Thursday review meeting. That will have to wait for another day.

I moved here to be closer to family, so I should get out of here and go visit Mom and Dad. I turn off the lights while there is still sun in the sky. It feels like a small success compared to my usual weekday routine of keeping hours from dark to dark.

Saturday afternoon finds me watching my niece play peewee hockey. There is nothing cuter than watching a scrum of little kids chase a hockey puck around the rink, no matter how cold the arena. Hockey is a favorite pastime in this part of the country, shall I even add, a rite of passage for every youngster. And it is every adult's rite of passage to freeze your backside on the metal bleachers.

My sister and I catch up on the week's events while keeping our eyes glued to the clump of kids moving in a gangly mess around the ice. I'm not sure which body is my niece in the knot of arms, legs, helmets, and hockey sticks.

I have always enjoyed watching hockey, even though I only

played a little when I was a youngster. I'm enjoying watching my niece. I've even been to our local high school game with my dad since I moved back. I watch some of the college games and even went to a few professional games when I lived in California. It seemed strange watching a sport like hockey in California, where it seems about as alien as birdwatching in the middle of the ocean.

My mind goes back to work, and I realize there are times when our Thursday meetings seem like the fights that break out during professional hockey games. I'm glad these kids aren't throwing down their gloves, pulling someone's jersey over their head, or giving someone the business while they turn hockey into some form of cage fighting. That saves a lot of premature dental work for our youngsters.

I continue to ponder the match and wonder why we don't have this kind of mayhem in the junior leagues. Look, I'm not advocating for fighting at this level, or any level for that matter. It occurs to me that the reason it doesn't happen is because they have rules—much stricter rules of conduct at this level, which become looser as you move up the ranks.

It makes me realize that what we need are more rules in our weekly review meetings. But that seems a bit overbearing. How do we put rules in place that protect everyone, but allow them to play freely?

HOW CAN WE CREATE BOUNDARIES SO THAT PEOPLE KNOW WHERE THEY ARE FREE TO PLAY WHEN IN CONFLICT?

My sister brings my attention back to the present moment, as it looks like her daughter just scored a goal. She admits the goal might have been as much accidental as intentional. But mother and daughter look ecstatic, and it doesn't really matter how it happened. It happened, and I got to see it.

It's time to stop thinking about work and enjoy these moments. I can think about the meeting rules later.

Chapter 2

Engaging Differently

On Sunday, my phone rings around one o'clock as I'm finishing my third coffee and planning what to do with my lazy day.

It's Carl. What a pleasant surprise. "To what do I owe the pleasure?"

"I was calling to compliment you on your definition. Thank you for sharing it with me."

"Gee, thanks for the call." I wonder if he had other intentions, but they aren't revealed right away if he had any at all. Instead, he seems genuinely interested.

After we talk through the definition, I share with him my reflections from yesterday's hockey match and the need for rules. I admit that rules seem heavy handed, but something has to be put in place to keep this group inside the guardrails.

He reminds me of someone we worked with during the early days of my previous employer who came in with a bunch of rules we had to follow in meetings. There was the baton passing, so that only the person with the baton could talk. And the timer for how long people could talk. He even had a penalty box where someone would pay a fine for bad meeting behaviors. If someone thought you were out of line, they could call it out and impose a fine, which was paid into a special fund.

I laugh as he recounts one of our more vocal teammates, who

took out a twenty-dollar bill to prepay his fine before he laid out Mr. Rules in spades. Needless to say, the rules and Mr. Rules didn't last long.

Carl says the group at our old company didn't need some set of rules because we had generally good habits when engaging each other in tough conversations. But it was not without effort. "Over time, the group developed norms that allowed us to deal with conflict. As new people joined the team, they learned from others. Or sometimes they provided new ways for us to engage with each other.

"Remember when John joined the team? When he was dealing with a difficult topic, he would ask for the group to divide and have one group argue for something and others argue against it. This quickly became another way we found to engage each other in healthy conflict, and as you wrote in your definition, to have 'deeper understanding.'"

The word "engage" jumps out at me, so I write it down, not knowing why or what purpose it will serve.

"In the military, they have rules of engagement. Should we come up with something like that?" I know the minute I ask the question that "rules" is the wrong word.

"Scratch that," I say. "'Rules' is too heavy handed. So are words like laws, edicts, and commandments. We need something that guides people and sets some boundaries."

There is a long, but not too uncomfortable, silence as we both sample possible words in our heads. Boundaries, procedures, guidelines, criteria, and statutes are all rifling through my brain as I sort through my best mental thesaurus. When I get to the word rubrics, I know I've gone too far. "It has to be simple," I say, and out of nowhere, the word pops out as I finish the sentence, "like principles. That's it! We need *principles of engagement* that guide us when we work together."

CAN WE DEFINE OUR PRINCIPLES OF ENGAGEMENT WHEN ENGAGING OTHERS, ESPECIALLY IN CONFLICT?

I can hear Carl's smile as he says, "I like it. Sounds like you have something to work with."

We finish up our call with some pleasantries, and Carl asks me to give him a call after Thursday's meeting. I know he is genuinely interested in what comes from this. I'm surprised and a little disappointed that he isn't hitting me up to come back to my former employer. I keep getting the sense there is a subtext to our connection, but that's probably just my imagination.

Well, it is Sunday, and time to finish my coffee and go enjoy some of the limited sun we get this time of year. I grab some hiking boots, my winter fleece, and a hat and head out the door. A quick hike, and then off to my parents' for dinner with the siblings, niece, and nephew.

I arrive at work for week five, and I'm quickly back in the throes of things long before the sun rises on Monday morning. I love the thrill of it; the adrenaline high is a real thing, and like a runner's high, it is the reward for the hard work. I spend the week planning and conspiring what to do with the weekly review meeting. I look at my definition on the whiteboard and use that as the basis for any changes.

CONFLICT: A GAP BETWEEN WHAT WE EXPECT AND WHAT WE EXPERIENCE THAT LEADS TO DEEPER UNDERSTANDING AND BETTER RESULTS.

In the end, we need to leverage the conflict, not avoid it. We need to leverage the collective knowledge, and we need to make decisions that get us better results.

At first, I think, *Get rid of the name of the meeting*. Could it sound any more boring? I don't have an alternative for now, so I stick a proverbial pin in that thought and agree to deal with it later.

HOW CAN WE LEVERAGE CONFLICT, NOT AVOID IT, TO LEVERAGE THE COLLECTIVE KNOWLEDGE AND ULTIMATELY MAKE DESCISIONS THAT GET US BETTER RESULTS?

The real issue is who attends the meeting. There are far too many people in the room. For the topics we discuss and the size of our company, the number ten, give or take, jumps out at me. I remember a university class that talked about optimal group size. There is plenty of debate and opinion about the right size. I'm not sure why, but ten feels like the right size. That means we will be cutting this meeting size by more than half.

Starting with who is in the meeting, I look at my checklist from the other day, where I noted that it is important to have those in the room who can make decisions. The operative word is "decisions." My first reaction is that this should be the VPs or directors, but that doesn't seem right. If that's the case, the company can never move unless the most senior people are in the room. I'm reminded of a quote from Steve Jobs:

"It doesn't make sense to hire smart people and tell them what to do; we hire smart people so they can tell us what to do."

This meeting can provide a development opportunity for the people running the day-to-day business to step forward and make decisions. As Steve Jobs said, we have hired smart people. Let's see what they tell us.

I realize the current mob mentality for the meeting attendees is creating conflict. Having the senior people make all the decisions causes everyone else in the meeting to defer, even when they know the answer from the senior employees is wrong. Afterward, they're all battling each other to make something work that they know is inherently wrong. It's like boundaries are drawn and there are battles between fiefdoms.

We don't want people to feel excluded, so I start by defining the core team. These are the people who can contribute productively to the meeting and help make decisions quickly on orders, forecasts, priorities, customer issues, etc. Everyone else is an alternate or substitute. They can attend the meeting if they feel compelled to or if one of the topics is relevant. They can attend part of the meeting or be on call if needed, or they can skip altogether.

I also organize the meeting into topics that need to be addressed. These are the areas where we have the greatest difficulty because they reflect the areas we end up in conflict. I come up with the following topics:

I.   Review previous week's orders
   □ Decision: any orders that need to be prioritized in the coming week(s)

II. Review any customer comments, complaints, or issues
   □ Decision: any actions needed to address customer needs

III. Review coming week's orders
   □ Decision: agree on order priorities for all new and existing orders

IV. Determine resources
   □ Decision: any resources or support needs between groups

V.   Discuss other topics
   □ Any other business items or topics

I tease myself that it's time to start surveying the battlefield. I begin by meeting with the key stakeholders, who are the VPs and directors, to socialize the attendees and decision points. Outside of some minor tweaks, the flow seems to fit. The focus on attendees is met with relief, with some people thanking me for giving them back their Thursday afternoons.

The only pushback I get is from Joanne, the head of operations, who tends to be a bit snarky. I had suggested one of her staff to be part of the core team. "Who do you think runs this ship?" she asks, and doesn't wait for an answer. "There isn't anything that goes through my shop I don't touch." Obviously, she instead thinks she is the core attendee. I can see her knuckles turning white as she grips the proverbial steering wheel.

Her need to be central to everything is what creates some of the biggest conflicts. But it isn't my job right now to convince her of the need to delegate and develop her team. She is more tenured, more senior, and more powerful than I am in the organization. This is not the hill I want to die on, so I acquiesce. Also, I still get the vibe she doesn't like me, and I'm thinking she doesn't trust me either. It reminds me that conflict doesn't have to be dealt with right in the moment. But it does need to be dealt with at some point.

With the feedback collected, I am ready to send out the meeting note. Rather than name the core team and meeting flow in the announcement, I plan to use the first meeting to review the recommendations, socialize the ideas, get any additional input, and ensure alignment. I also plan to let the team come up with a new name for the meeting.

On Wednesday night, I see Carolyn.

I review my plan for the meeting attendees and flow, as well as how I plan to socialize it with the group. There is something in her gaze that makes me think I'm missing something, and that she might be hesitant to point it out. So I ask.

She says, "I like your plan, and I'm sure it will help with the soul sapping you shared with me. I'm just wondering about the conflict as you defined it. Do you think this approach will increase conflict or reduce it?"

I frown a little, like a grammar schooler who just had her work corrected after she thought she did a good job.

"I'm not saying it's a showstopper or that you should change the meeting approach. I'm just thinking about where you started the first time we talked, which was with conflict and how that was creating the challenge in this meeting."

I brighten up a bit. "I'm with you. How good is my definition of conflict, if I'm the only one who sees it? And if I believe this to be fundamental to what is happening in the meeting, and the organization, why wouldn't I open the meeting with this so we have a basis to talk about conflict?"

"I like your thinking," Carolyn says as she pops up and bounces on with her building rounds. "Let me know how it goes!" echoes behind her as she exits my office and heads down the hallway.

IS THERE A BETTER DEFINITION OF CONFLICT?

I like that woman, I think as I realize she and I are probably the last ones in the building. *I need to make an effort to leave a little earlier, but our conversations are a reward for the longer day.*

Chapter 3

Aligning the Team

Thursday is here and the afternoon brings the weekly review meeting to the forefront. I show up a few minutes before 1:00 p.m. and I'm the first to arrive. The second person doesn't arrive until five minutes after, and it's 1:30 before we have any kind of quorum. The good news is that the earlier arrivals are those who have been identified as core attendees. The rest can play catch-up when they get there, so I start the meeting.

I start by sharing my personal experience and reflections. "I have to admit I've been struggling with this meeting since I started here. There were so many things challenging me. For example, we seemed to lack clear decisions, or alignment around decisions. There seem to be things under the surface that are keeping us from working together, and the meeting itself seems to lack form, function, or structure."

I see lots of heads nodding, but I am also sensitive because I could be calling someone's baby ugly. I see Joanne's face scouring and think it could be her baby. I continue on and try to recover.

"Getting together is important to us, to our business, and most importantly, to our customers. We need to make decisions, and we need to leverage all the perspectives in the room. So I am not saying this is a bad idea or we should stop meeting. We may need to refine the focus.

"Last week I got 'volun-told' to run this meeting." ("Volun-told" is a funny word combining volunteering and being told that we used when I was a kid and our parents volunteered us for something without an option.)

Everyone chuckled. "I know I'm the newest to the team, and I may not see everything the way you do. I have some ideas I want to share and get your input on.

"First, I want to talk about conflict and what it means to us. I was talking with someone and thought the underlying problem was conflict. However, over the past week, I don't think conflict is our problem; it is by nature a necessary and inherent part of what we do. We will always be in conflict. So I was challenged to redefine what conflict means for me, for us, and for our business. This is what I came up with."

I turn over the flip chart page to reveal the definition I had written.

CONFLICT: A GAP BETWEEN WHAT WE <u>EXPECT</u> AND WHAT WE <u>EXPERIENCE</u> THAT LEADS TO DEEPER <u>UNDERSTANDING</u> AND BETTER <u>RESULTS</u>.

I focus my attention on the word "gap" and explain that managing these gaps is central to what we are doing in this meeting. "We will frequently have gaps to contend with, like lack of resources, different priorities, and any other host of challenges."

I also talk about how we need to make sure we gain the perspectives of everyone in the room. That by doing so we can get smarter and make better decisions. "I know there are times we're not seeing the full picture because we don't ask for others' perspectives or people might be hesitant to speak up. We can see it in the hallway conversations after the meeting and the problems that keep resurfacing. If we can get a better perspective, ultimately this will help us drive better results." I wrap up my sermon by saying that I hope we can work better to close some of these gaps.

I don't get an amen, round of applause, or standing ovation, but the nods suggest that I'm on the right track. So it's time to pivot to the meeting format.

I review the key agenda items and emphasize the necessity of using this meeting to make decisions. The focus on decisions seems to amp up the energy in the room, and I realize making decisions is very high-energy and motivates people. The failure to make decisions is what saps peoples' energy.

Dominic, the manager of IT, speaks up. "What if we can't make a decision in this meeting?" Dom tends to be one of the team members who throws barriers to see if people can jump over them.

MAKING DECISIONS IS HIGH-ENERGY; FAILURE TO MAKE DECISIONS IS WHAT SAPS ENERGY.

Bill, the company controller, takes a shot across Dominic's bow. "There goes IT again, always looking for the problems." I've heard that Bill and Dom are known for butting heads.

I take a breath and say, "Rather than seeing Dom as an obstructionist, maybe he is pointing out a gap we need to manage. Isn't that what causes some of these challenges?" Hmm, this definition might truly help us manage conflict.

Rather than take the bait of responding, I put it back to the group. "What do you all think about situations where we might not be able to make a decision here?"

After some uncomfortable silence, Kim, one of the supervisors from my team, speaks up. "It seems there will be plenty of decisions we may not be able to make in this room. Maybe we should first ask ourselves, 'Can we make a decision?'"

Surprisingly, Joanne jumps in using her direct tone of voice. "Sometimes we hamstring ourselves by assuming we can't make the decision when we can. In those cases, we should just make the decision and move on." Her direct style is helpful in situations like this.

Dom says, "Okay, what if the answer is no, we can't make the decision. For example, I need two more programmers on my team to get all the work done. What should we do then?"

I remind myself that he is naming a gap. "Then maybe we look where we might have control. For example, on the resource scenario, we may not be able to decide to add resources in this meeting, but we might be able to decide on how we prioritize our work to minimize the burden on the resources we have."

Dom seems to reluctantly accept that. But we aren't done yet— Sally, our manager of sales operations, puts the icing on the cake when she says, "Or maybe the decision for this group is how we can elevate the issue in the most effective way to get resource help. It seems to me that sometimes we don't elevate the issue because we think the answer will be no, or we don't elevate it with a strong case for why we need something."

That was a good exchange and discussion. It jumps out at me that, with the exception of Joanne, all of that discussion came from people who weren't most senior in the room. Also, they're the key people I thought should be in the weekly meeting.

I transition to talk about who is in the meeting and the idea of alternates. I talk about the ability of and need for those managing the front line of the business to take on more decisions. I notice my stakeholders nodding, even Joanne.

I list off the core team of nine, starting with myself, manager of customer service; Sally, manager of sales operations; Bill, controller; Dom, IT supervisor; Joanne, VP of operations; Jim, manager of logistics; LaDonna, engineering manager; Dino, plant and maintenance manager; and Kim, who works for me and is a customer service supervisor. I feel that having Kim from my team will keep me from wearing two hats: meeting leader and manager of customer service. It also provides a development opportunity for Kim.

Peter, the sales VP, speaks up. He loves to poke at the belly of the beast. "Hey Joanne, why are you in this meeting? Don't you have other things you can be doing?" He says it with a smile, which is part of the reason he can get away with this comment. The other is that he has been at the company longer than Joanne, and is the only one who can say something like this. I, for one, am glad he brought it up.

Joanne is none too pleased to be challenged, and her neck turns flush red. I think a vein is bulging in her temple. It's a stark contrast to Peter's inviting smile.

She fires a shot back at Peter. "Operations keeps the trains running on time. I need to be here to make sure all of your frequent rush orders get done."

Peter does his usual disarming chuckle and smiles, ever the charmer. "I get you, Joanne. I would only suggest that we are all putting people from our teams at the center of this meeting. Maybe it is an opportunity for you to get some things off of your plate."

As he says this, Gordie, one of the operations managers from Joanne's team, sits forward but says nothing. It catches Joanne's eye, and she says, "Fine, lets add Gordie to the core team." Gordie smiles, knowing this is a good move for him. She turns to me and says, "Does that throw off your grand design, Angela?"

I ignore her jab. "Nope, I'm good." I smile, and with that, the topic is closed and one of my concerns is partially resolved. I know I am going to owe Peter again.

Dom speaks up again. "What if we need one of the VPs to be in the room to make a decision."

"I have agreement from our sponsors"—what I am calling the directors and VPs—"to be available and willing to take calls on a Thursday afternoon if there is something urgent. Also, as we plan the weekly agenda, if there is something we need them for at that week's meeting, someone can ask them to come for that segment." I add one last note of inclusion. "And of course, they are welcome to attend any meeting they want, we aren't excluding them. What we want to accomplish is having a core group that can make decisions and resolve any gaps." I congratulate myself on working my key word "gap" from the definition of conflict into the conversation.

As I review the recommended agenda, I ask the group if we are all willing to commit to starting on time. "If we can start promptly at 1:00 p.m., I will ensure we end promptly at 5:00 p.m." I see as much skepticism in their eyes as I feel in my gut. I'm not quite sure how I will keep to the promise to adjourn on time.

Having gained some tacit buy-in to the meeting framework, I add one last request. "Weekly review meeting, although descriptive, might not represent what we are trying to accomplish, nor does it sound like a movie I would want to see. Can I ask the group to bring recommendations for the name to next week's meeting?" Part of the goal in renaming the meeting is to breathe some life into this, but also, names are important. A new name might help bring new meaning and focus.

With that done, I recommend we move into the meeting agenda. I welcome anyone to stay who would like to, but only those on the core team list are required.

I am glad to see most of the non-core members leave the meeting.

As we start the formal meeting, I direct our attention to the decision points I had scribed onto the flip chart.

I. Review previous week's orders
    ☐ Decision: any orders that need to be prioritized in the coming week(s)

II. Review any customer comments, complaints, or issues
    ☐ Decision: any actions needed to address customer needs

III. Review coming week's orders
    ☐ Decision: agree on order priorities for all new and existing orders

IV. Determine resources
    ☐ Decision: any resources or support needs between groups

V. Discuss other topics
    ☐ Any other business items or topics

The sounding bell rings and we are off to the races. And with all my good intentions, the meeting quickly devolves into a scrum, just like my niece's peewee hockey. Someone lobs in their urgent topic of the day while others try to wrestle attention away to another urgent topic of the day. I try to work in an orderly manner using the decision point of last week's orders review. That gets knocked out of bounds because I am reminded that last week's missed orders are what we need to prioritize this week's orders. That then turns into a conversation about a customer call for a late order that had already shipped.

We get through a number of topics, but only a few are resolved. The group seems demoralized and bloodied. Another meeting, and wounded soldiers are limping out of the room. I keep my commitment to end at five, more as a declaration of defeat than a victory of keeping to my commitment. We adjourn and I stay in the conference room, exhausted and drained again. My niece's peewee hockey team seems better organized.

As I sit there licking my wounds, Carolyn comes bounding in doing her building rounds. Someone else is doing the regular cleaning work—Carolyn is on another mission—but I don't know what it is. When I ask what brings her in today, she says she is shadowing her team to see how they are doing and what they need.

Although I love her energy, today it wears me down even more. She asks how the meeting went. I'm sure she sees some of my defeat on my face, in my eyes, and from my posture.

I realize it wasn't all bad, and it's good to share the success of resetting the meeting focus and attendees. Also, I thank her for reminding me to think about my definition of conflict. I tell her that I think the definition seems to help shift the team's thinking.

I share Dom's comment and how previously I (and probably others) would have seen it as obstructionist. However, using Dom's comment to highlight a gap ended up generating a better discussion.

"That seems like a good outcome, so why do you look dejected?" she asks.

I share with her how the meeting quickly devolved when we tried to work together. She nods and empathizes. "I know that feeling," she says. "It seems that the more conversation we have, the more confusion we create." She lets that sit for a minute while I try to shake the fog from my head.

> **ONE OF OUR RESPONSIBILITIES AS LEADERS IS TO ENGINEER THE CONVERSATIONS FOR OUR ORGANIZATION.**

She continues, "I think one of our responsibilities as leaders is to engineer the conversations necessary for our organizations."

That sounds like a strange choice of words. "Engineer the conversations?" I say, emphasizing the word "engineer."

"Yes. We tend to think of conversations as something open-ended, nebulous, and amorphous. Something that we do, and at times without structure or clear purpose. Have you ever walked out of a conversation that covered nothing and accomplished nothing?"

"I usually regret those because they represent minutes or hours I will never get back." I smile slightly.

She continues. "At the end of the day, all you're doing is having conversations. You can have the best systems, the best processes, the best products, but if you can't engage in robust conversation, you aren't going anywhere. There is a way to 'engineer' the conversations to create better clarity, understanding, and results. This is especially true when you're in conflict, and as we have discussed, we spend most of our time managing conflict."

An idea forms in my head as she is talking and the fog starts to clear. I say, "Conversation is our universal leadership tool."

Carolyn smiles and nods in agreement. "The key is to have an approach that allows you to have those conversations. That is why you have the scrum, as you call it. When I think of 'engineering the conversation,' it reminds me there's a method to what can at times feel like madness."

The light starts to shine in my mind, and off Carolyn goes bounding into the evening. Her voice echoes down the hall: "Remember, it is your job to engineer the conversations necessary for the company's results."

I gather my things and head back to my office to sort through the mess from today's meeting, but more importantly, the mess of conversations we had today.

When I get to the office, my phone is ringing, and without looking at the screen, I know it's Carl.

"So . . . ?" he asks, letting the question finish itself.

I fill him in on the meeting, repeating much of what I shared with Carolyn. I also include the discussion about engineering the conversations for the organization, realizing that is part of the challenge I'm facing.

Carl had the same reaction to the term "engineering the conversation," but we both agree there is some merit to the word choice. As an engineer by trade, he likes the idea that there can be a method to process information more effectively. He also likes the point that it is our responsibility as leaders to engineer the necessary conversations. As we talk, I go to the whiteboard and write in the upper righthand corner:

> *It is our responsibility to engineer the necessary conversations.*

"Since we are a fairly technical organization, I think that word could resonate for many of the people here." I laugh at myself. "Even for me, the anti-engineer," as Carl used to teasingly call me.

Carl pipes back, "Don't forget all of your background as a systems analyst. You have that eye for process. Plus, I think everyone has an ability to see things systematically. When we get a good system in place, it doesn't matter what your background is, it just makes sense."

I agree as I think of Peter, our consummate salesperson. I'm sure he has a system or method for engaging in conversations when he is working with clients and negotiating deals, whether he recognizes it or not.

CAN WE CREATE A MORE DELIBERATE WAY TO HAVE CONVERSATIONS?

Carl has to run, as he has another meeting before the end of his day and I need to bring my day to a close. We say our goodbyes and off we go. I'm appreciating these conversations with Carolyn and Carl. They help me to clear my head and give me things to think about. As I drive home, the words "engineer the conversations" reverberate through my head. That will need some thinking.

Chapter 4

IdEA Model

The next morning, the idea of "engineering the conversations" continues to swirl in my brain like a fine wine breathing before it is consumed. I know the thought invaded my dreams because quick flashes keep coming back to me. They are a series of dream fragments that don't seem to make sense, but I keep trying to put them together to see what they mean.

I have flashes of all these conversations I need to have each day, I have flickers of our team meetings, individual meetings with my teammates, and even phone calls with customers. But they're jumbled in with images of the production floor at work. I can see stacks of crates on one end of the floor, a bunch of people bustling about the floor, and then pallets being loaded onto trucks on the other end of the floor.

The minute I try to put my dreams out of my mind, another fragment blazes across my brain like a movie clip from some unknown film. It has an almost surreal feeling.

When I get to the office, I decide to walk through the production area. I enter through the back door, which is usually reserved for those involved in production. Production is up and humming along since they run two shifts a day. I get some glances, as I'm sure some are wondering if I'm some kind of lost interloper.

For some reason I can't explain, I'm drawn to this area. It's like some mysterious force from last night's weird dream is pulling me here. Like the key to my fragmented dream is to be found in this vast expanse of building and fabricating.

The production area is actually an old airplane hangar left over from World War II when midsized bombers were manufactured here. The space has been totally revamped and has a much more sleek, modern, and technological feel to it than in the days of steel sheets and rivets.

I take a casual stroll over to a set of stairs leading to an old catwalk still hanging over the production area. I'm probably one of the few interlopers this vestige of a day gone by has seen in some time. The catwalk is nearly two full stories above the floor and well above the bright lights that hang over the production area. I get a full view of the stream of activity from arriving materials to my right, production below me, and shipping to the left.

There's a smooth flow to the process, even though I can't tell specifically what each work pod performs. Someone engineered all this to work together, an impressive piece of work.

As I lean over the railing watching what's happening, the word "engineering" pops back into my mind. This production area is as much an engineering feat today as it was over seventy years ago. This plant made a sizable contribution to the 265 planes produced in the US per day during the peak of the war production. Today it produces high-tech products used in many companies around the world. The process back then was probably the same then as it is today. Things come in, people do something to that stuff, and things go out the other end.

I gaze out, letting the rhythm of the flow wash over me. Things come in, things are being worked on, things go out. My dream from last night comes back to me in another of those flashes, reminding me how the production floor and conversations were jumbled together.

Carolyn's words from yesterday echo in my head: "Remember, it is your job to engineer the conversations necessary for the company's results."

Can I engineer conversations with the same kind of flow I see on the floor below me? Although there a lots of moving parts, there are really only three things happening. Again I focus on the rhythm of the production floor. *Things come in, people do something to that stuff, and things go out the other end.*

I start to see why these two things invaded my brain. I see the connection between engineering a production flow and Carolyn's comment about engineering the conversations. I descend the stairs from the catwalk to head back to my office. First, because I've goofed off long enough, but also to capture my thoughts before they flit away like my dream fragments.

When I get to the office, I start to write on the whiteboard a pictogram of how we might engineer conversations. I can't help adding a creative flare, so I shade in my loops.

So production has three things happening: raw materials come in, something gets done to that material, and things go out the other end. So what are the three things that happen in a conversation?

The first is pretty easy. In some way, a topic gets introduced, which tells us what we are working on. That is what we bring into a conversation. It seems it might be bigger than just the topic. We might have something we want to talk about, a topic, but there is a manner in which we find clarity about that topic. Instead of "Topic," I write, "Identify." It occurs to me that although we cover many topics, we don't always clearly "Identify" the actual topic. It seems that "Identify" fits better, although I'm not quite sure why just yet. So I write that at the top of our process.

I reflect how, when someone raises a topic, everyone tends to jump in with ideas, opinions, and suggestions as soon as the discussion starts. That seems to fit better at the end of the process, with what goes out. Our hope is that we have some kind of action or decision from the conversation. And hope we do, even if it is unlikely in too many cases. So at the end I write, "Action."

The middle is a big blank. What goes in here? It's kind of like the manufacturing floor I was watching this morning. Lots of different activities are going on to convert the raw material into something that gets shipped. Can we define the activities that help convert the topic into some kind of action?

I'm reflecting on our meeting and my frustration when everyone would jump in on a topic before understanding it fully. It's frustrating because I also do the same thing. I can't help myself, and I'm sure others have the same challenge. But this is where the opportunity is to have a better product, the actual actions we take.

The void in the middle is taunting me. I stare at the whiteboard for what seems like an eternity. It isn't that long, it just seems like forever.

What would be better than jumping in too soon with a solution? What would work in the middle to create better outcomes?

EXPLORING AND UNDERSTANDING ARE CENTRAL TO MANAGING CONFLICT.

I snap out of my gaze to write a question mark next to that middle part of the process. Not because I don't know, but because I think we can do much better by asking more questions. This is what can drive the middle of our definition: "To get deeper understanding."

That's it, my little brainstorm, or at least a light misting, as my friend Carl teasingly calls it. I'm thinking of a word that would fit for the question mark when I realize we need to do a better job "exploring" topics before we jump to a conclusion, so I write that on the whiteboard.

I realize we don't ask questions, we don't seek others' points of view, we talk over other people's ideas, we shut out others who don't see things the way we do, and we even hijack one topic to push our agenda on something else entirely. In the context of our definition of conflict as a gap, we don't get to the point where we try to understand the gap. If we are going to engineer better conversations, we need to do a much better job of processing or exploring.

— ∞ —

As I'm looking at my little drawing, Dino, our plant and maintenance manager, comes in for a quick question. He sits down and glances up at my whiteboard, seeing my simple drawing under the phrase "Engineer the conversations necessary for the organizations success." He asks what that all means and I explain, in short form, what came from the conversation with Carolyn and my idea from this morning.

"I wondered why you were wandering around the plant this morning. So tell me more about what you're thinking," he says.

I focus first on Identify, or the raw materials of our conversations. We both agree that we tend to heap topics into messy piles, never really deciding what we are going to talk about.

He says, "It would be the equivalent of manufacturing receiving random shipments of material without thinking about what they want to produce."

"That's why our conversations feel like a game of whack-a-mole," I say, reflecting on the game my niece and nephew played on our last trip to Chuck E. Cheese. It's the kids game where you use a mallet to pound down a mole in one hole, and another pops up out of another hole.

He agrees. "That's why our meetings are as exhausting as taking kids to that overstimulated jungle of sugar and adrenaline."

Dino shares his experience from one of his graduate classes. He says that one of our core skills as leaders is to "frame" topics to create focus. He explains that framing not only creates focus, but sets the stage for conversations.

I go to the whiteboard and write next to the Identify block "Focus Framing."

FRAMING IS A CORE CONVERSATIONAL SKILL.

"The challenge is doing so succinctly." He explains how hard it can be to narrow something down to the essence of what you want to discuss. "It seems we don't spend enough time really defining what we are talking about. Someone brings something up, and everyone pulls the topic in different directions. I like that you've identified this is a core part of our conversations, because we seem to fail to get off on the right foot in our meetings."

After a little more discussion, I remember that Dino had come to me with a question, so I pivot back to him so I don't take too much of his time. After talking through a challenge he is having and some help he needs from my group, we break and he heads out, leaving me alone with my thoughts.

After my conversation with Dino, I look up at the loops on my whiteboard and realize I still haven't mapped out the conversation. I reflect on what I noticed in production, that "things come in, people do something to that stuff, and things go out the other end." I have now mapped conversations in the same way. What comes in is Identify. Where people do something with that stuff is Explore. But what comes out the other end of a conversation?

I flash back to the conversations I used to have with an old colleague. We talked about lots of stuff and explored lots of stuff, but each talk felt meaningless. These conversations were like a bad movie where you walk out and think, *There goes two hours of my life I'm never going to get back.* Sure, we talked a lot, but what was missing? Why did our conversations feel so empty, even though they were filled with lots of words?

I've been looking at the whiteboard for what seems like an eternity, and the hole in the last part of the loop is shouting for my attention. Time comes to a stop. An idea is drumming in the back of my mind. It's soft at first and hard to hear. Then it starts reverberating louder, until it's shouting in my brain.

I finally see the connection between what comes out at the end of our production process and what comes out from a good conversation. It's what was missing in those empty conversations with my colleague. It's what causes us to feel an emptiness after a conversation.

I grab my marker and fill in the last part of my loops on the white-board, and then cap the marker like I'm putting a period at the end of a sentence. I take one last look at the loop as I turn off the light and head out the door with the satisfaction that comes from getting clarity.

The IdEA Conversational Framework

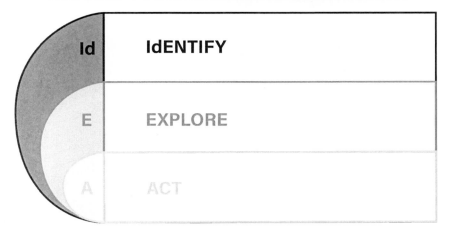

As I drive home, I think about the conversational loop with Identify, Explore, and Act. What should I call it? I toss around the words in my head to see what falls out, like a mental game or word scramble. I'm a bit distracted and nearly drive through a red light. As I slam on my brakes, all the letters and words jumble again, only this time an interesting mnemonic pops out. Using the first letters of each word, with a little liberty, I spell out "idea": a capital I for Identify, E for Explore, and A for Act. Including the "d" from identi-fy, we can call it the IdEA Model. So I don't risk violating any more traffic laws, I file the name away in my memory bank with the intent of writing it on the whiteboard in the morning. The rest of my drive home is relaxing as the twinkle of streetlights, brake lights, head-lights, and front porch lights wash over me.

Chapter 5

The Topic-Briefing Template

As I finish up my thought on the whiteboard ready to dive into the crisis of the day when Peter, our VP of sales, comes in. I think to myself, *He is here to collect the debt of protecting me from Joanne in the meeting.*

He grabs a seat at the table and sets a coffee in front of me. "For you," he says. I notice that it's the proper tan color and the appropriate smell of sweetness. This guy is good; he knows how to win you over. Not only does he bring me coffee, but he knows the right amount of cream and sugar. I release myself from the wafting aroma to realize, oh my, he really does want something now.

But rather than ask for something, he starts checking in on yesterday's meeting. He compliments me on how I handled it, the new flow, and the trimmed attendee list. He even thanks me for giving him back a few hours a week. He is also pretty effusive about the definition of the conflict as a gap and getting the team to focus on closing the gap. "So how do you propose to get them closing the gap?" It's a sincere inquiry, not a challenge or gotcha.

"I'm not quite sure yet." I share with him my thinking around the three pieces of the conversation I had written on the whiteboard. He nods with that approving frown someone gives you when they mean "Nice job."

"I like it, because it is simple and elegant. I'm a simple kind of guy, so I would get it." He continues, "So how do we get people to 'identify' the gap?"

"I'm not sure." I feel stuck.

Peter picks up the thread of the conversation. "I remember meetings in my former life before I worked in this business. It seems like people would throw out comments or issues like cow pies and leave them there for others to deal with. Oftentimes no one knew what they were talking about, why they were talking about it, or what they wanted to happen."

Peter continues: "I think it's natural for people to see what they perceive as a problem, but not define it clearly or know what they want."

"We aren't good at naming the gap," I say.

"Sounds about right. Sounds like you identified the gap in your gap!"

I grab a marker from the whiteboard and jot a note under my definition.

NAME THE GAP.

"So how do we name it better?" I ask out loud, as much for his benefit as my own.

"Let's use your challenge with the team not being able to clearly name the gap to find a way to name the gap," he says, amused by his twist on the words.

"I don't know how to name it. It's like a fog is hanging over the battlefield of our meeting, obscuring everything."

"Let's ask a few questions first. Share with me everything you see, hear, and experience in this meeting."

I start to unload a bunch of stuff in no particular order. I share things I hear like the engineers are holding us back, sales is so high maintenance, IT won't help with anything. He is nice enough to let that slight at the sales group slide by.

Peter says, "Most of what you shared doesn't describe the problems; they are more accusations."

I continue his sentence. "And they don't share any information about what's causing it. No one takes ownership, and worse, they don't even say what they want."

Peter says, "It sounds like people aren't putting a name on topics that is helpful or productive."

He walks over to the whiteboard and jots some notes:

NAME IT
RELEVANT BACKGROUND
THE ASK

"When I meet with the senior staff or with a customer, I try to provide three things. First, regardless of what I am talking about, I need to be able to name it in a way that is clear and concise, one or two simple sentences. That seems easy, but as you're finding out right now, it can be hard to do.

"Sometimes I start with the second thing I wrote up here, 'Relevant background.' Sometimes it helps me to list out all the background I can think of, get it out there so I can look at it, see it, organize it, focus it. But when I'm bringing a topic forward, I need to cull it down to the most relevant background." He emphasizes *most relevant*. "Oftentimes we wash over people with way too much information, and in the process, we lose them.

> **OUR ABILITY TO "FRAME" A TOPIC IS A CORE LEADERSHIP SKILL.**

"The third thing is 'What is my ask?' If I don't know what I'm asking for, how will they? And I can promise you, if you don't know what you're asking, you're guaranteed to never get it.

"As you grow as a leader, you will find that your ability to frame is really key to your success. And that is what we are talking about: framing skills."

I like the simple format he has written on the whiteboard.

He draws a bracket next to it, connecting this simple format to the "Identify" in my conversational process. "This might provide a simple way for you and the others to frame topics more effectively and create focus in the conversation."

I pick up a marker and write "Frame and Focus" next to the "Identify" of my conversational process.

I can see now why he is a successful salesperson. He's a charmer, he listens to people, he's smart, and he can net things out in a simple way.

He brings it back to our original discussion about the meeting. "So if you were to name the gap you're experiencing in your meeting, how would you use this to name it more succinctly?"

With all my years of education, my command of the English language, and Peter's tutorial, all I can come up with is "It's a mess."

He smiles and suggests we start in the middle first, with Relevant background.

I start rattling off bullets of things I've seen and observed, like lack of clarity, not considering broader perspectives, using words that put others on the defensive, the rabbit-hole scenario, where we dive down a rabbit hole of a topic with no resolve, and the whack-a-mole scenario, where we tend to jump around too much without resolving any one topic. Also, I realize how even if someone tries to organize his or her thoughts, someone will jump in and hijack the conversation without ever knowing what the person wants. Lastly, if someone brings something up, we have to understand why they are bringing it up and what they want from the conversation.

After several minutes of my rambling he asks, "So what would you call that?"

"A failure to clearly name a challenge or opportunity, with no clear ownership or resolution." I'm shocked that it just pops out of my mouth. I guess starting with the background helped me put a name on it better. That messiness created some clarity.

"So it sounds like you've named it, and covered the most relevant background," he continues. "What do you want?"

"I want to have us do a better job of clearly and succinctly naming a challenge or opportunity." I explain my use of challenge and opportunity, because I don't want it to always be about a problem. "But I want more than that." I smile.

Peter says, "Of course you do."

"I want an approach we can use to raise a topic; I want us to do it efficiently and also in a way that encourages others to share their perspectives. And oh yeah, for the cherry on top, I would like to have someone take ownership."

Peter asks, "What if the person who raises the topic doesn't have control over the topic?"

"I think it's more about owning the topic and leading the discussion than owning the outcome. Also, I would assume that many times, there are multiple owners who need to take action. I just want to get us out of the lobbing hand-grenade game and leaving it to others."

"Sounds like you have a clear statement to name your gap," he says.

"Maybe that's part of the solution. I can see if the approach you've given me here will help people do that better." I add, "If someone raises a topic for discussion, do I have them fill it out before the meeting?"

Peter expels a "Hmm" as he lets me answer my own question.

I continue by accepting the implied invitation. "Well, if they know in advance, they can use this to get ready for the meeting. But if something comes up in the meeting, I don't see why they can't outline their talking points before they bring it up," I say, thinking of the more introverted members of the team who may want time to organize their thoughts. "But if someone wants to lob a bombshell, they can use this outline to organize what they're going to say."

"Are you going to give them a time limit?" he asks.

"No, but I will suggest that they should be able to walk through something in a few minutes."

"What about those folks who love to have a PowerPoint of a few hundred slides?" he challenges me, knowing there are some people who love their slides full of bullet points and use them like a tele-prompter as if they're giving a presidential speech.

"Other than retraining them on presentation skills, we can suggest that the key points from the outline be the first slide so everyone knows where we are going with a topic."

"So if you're to use what you just came up with as a way to name the gap, as you so eloquently defined it, how would you tee this up with the team?"

"I would start by sharing with them that I want to talk about how we identify opportunities and challenges in a more succinct way that keeps us focused on the gap and ensures we have actionable outcomes. I would share a few of the examples of the things we discussed, but not all of them. I'm sure they will get it."

"And your ask from the group is?"

"I want to get their input on the approach we've outlined here, and their agreement on using an approach we can use in future meetings."

"Sounds to me like you have succinctly identified your gap. Remember, you aren't just handing this to them as a fully baked meal. You're giving them a starting point. They will want, and should have an opportunity, to share thoughts and ideas." He points to "Explore" in my conversational process. "And you never know, they could have a better way," he says as he points to "Action."

"One last thought for you," he says as he heads for the doorway. "Use your top box and bottom box as your guardrails. That will keep your conversation on track. It might help you manage the rabbit holes, the whack-a-mole, and the other challenges you mentioned."

I look at him, puzzled, for a minute until I realize he has drawn the three items—Name it, Relevant background, and The Ask—in a boxed form. The top box is Name it and the bottom box is The Ask.

That makes sense that they would serve as the guardrails for any conversation.

Once Peter is gone, I quickly open a document to capture my thoughts and start outlining my notes for our next meeting. I think the team will like something with a defined format, since so many of them come from technical fields.

So I put a title on it: Topic-Briefing Template (TBT). I put a subtitle underneath, borrowing an pneumonic from an old boss. He used to tell us that when we come to him with something, we should BLUF, which stands for Bottom Line Up Front.

When I'm done, I have a one-page template that I think will at least give us a starting point, and I've used it for a topic we need to discuss as a team.

Topic-Briefing Template
Bluf: Bottom Line Upfront

TOPIC NAME	
BACKGROUND	
OUTCOME—"THE ASK"	

I'm eager to try it out, so I head off to sit with Kim from my team, whom I know has some challenges we need to address in the next meeting. I walk her through the template and ask if she would be willing to work with me to outline one of her challenges. She eagerly jumps in on a pretty hot topic.

"We have an order from a major customer that has been delayed three weeks in a row. Every time we think we have resolved it, we show up the next week and something else has happened. The first week, software engineering had to make a last-minute change to customize something the client wanted. This wasn't documented in the statement of work, but the salesperson makes a case for this as a 'have to have.' The next week, quality assurance held it up because it hadn't been fully tested and documented. Last week, sales came in with another tweak the customer wanted. This week, we were about to ship again," she says with exasperation, "when someone realized we didn't have the updated shipping information and complete delivery instructions."

She continues talking and now adds in other occurrences of the same things happening with other customers. It's starting to sound like one of those whack-a-mole conversations that happen in our weekly meetings.

After more venting, Kim says, "This isn't about this order, it's bigger than that."

I sit back and let her continue to think and talk. Finally she says, "The problem is really about how we handle special requests from clients. We handle standard orders pretty well, but the minute we try to be responsive to unique customer needs, we end up with problems that impact not only those orders, but all the other orders we are working on. When we push back, we get the 'we need to be responsive to customers if we are going to stay in business' lecture from the sales team."

After a lengthy discussion, Kim has actually written out the topic using the TBT. She has a clear statement at the top and has done a good job outlining the most relevant background.

To finish it off, I ask, "So what do you want from the group?"

"I want it fixed," she says, knowing that isn't a clear enough ask. "I think I want, or we need, two things. First, we have to figure out how we're going to handle these special orders right now. It's causing too much disruption. Second, we have to figure out a standard method to handle special orders in a way we don't have to jump through all these hoops.

"But I can't own this—it's way too big, there's too much I can't control, and everyone has a handprint on this crime scene," she continues.

"For now, would you be comfortable owning the topic? To be the person to bring it to the group, get us talking about it, and help at least define next steps?" I ask.

LEADING THE TOPIC DOESN'T REQUIRE YOU TO OWN ALL THE ACTION.

Her shoulders unclench and her breathing returns to a more normal rate. I know her yes is sincere, and she feels confident bringing it up in our next meeting.

I use any free time before our next meeting to review the TBT idea with the core team members to get their input. Generally, the idea is well received and I get some helpful feedback. For example, I get more ideas on how to outline a topic and when to use the TBT. Several want it available electronically. And Dom, who usually challenges ideas, is very supportive and suggests we have printed copies at the meeting for people to take notes if they are preparing something on the fly.

One of the meetings is with Joanne, and I'm not looking forward to it. I actually wait until the day before the review meeting to see her. I still get the feeling she doesn't like me personally, and she may be an obstructionist to any change to the meetings.

I sit down with her early in the morning when we are two of

the first few to the office. I hope that by meeting with her outside the throes of the daily chaos, we might have a better conversation. When I walk into the office, her body language is fairly closed off. She is in her chair, arms crossed, shoulders arched forward, and head titled down as she looks over the top of her glasses. That look reminds me of my crotchety old uncle. She looks ready to pounce.

For the first time, our conversation isn't all business. Don't get me wrong, we aren't talking about personal lives and family. It starts by her asking how I found my office, to which she shares how hers drives her crazy. It's loud because it's near the shipping end of the production area, and often freezing cold. I guess I would be a little cranky too if I had to work in that type of environment. That could explain some of her moods. It hits me that her posture isn't because of me—the woman is cold. As she looks down at the document I brought, she is looking through her glasses, which are readers. She wasn't looking over her glasses in judgment; she had to, because if she looked at me through the readers, I would probably look all distorted like a Picasso painting.

We get down to business fairly quickly, and I'm a little more relaxed after realizing all the signals she sent weren't necessarily accurate. I'm still a bit guarded because I have seen and been on the receiving end of the scrapes from her sharp edges.

I walk her through the TBT process. She listens intently, and I can't determine whether she is ready to pounce or genuinely interested in the approach. I tell myself to assume the later. I can see why the meetings are edgy, because no one can tell.

After I finish, she sits a little more forward in her chair and asks a few questions like:

"How do you expect people to prepare?"

"What if they can't impact the topic they raise?"

"Isn't this going to make the meeting overly structured?"

"How do you determine what topics you are going to work on in any given meeting? We can't cover everything."

I realize her natural speaking style comes out abrupt, and it can make me, and others, naturally defensive. I let it roll off my shoulders and share with her some of our thinking on the approach. She nods with approval. I hadn't thought about how to handle it if we have too many topics and how to prioritize who gets airtime.

Joanne suggests that if we have too many topics, we let the group pick what they want to work on. Very democratic of her.

Her question about being overly structured gives me something to think about. I thank her for that and let her know I will think about it and how to make sure we have a good flow.

When we're done and as I get ready to leave, she thanks me. I almost fall over the chair. I hope she doesn't notice the trip or my shock.

"I think it's good that you keep socializing these things with me and the rest of the group."

Her word choice is interesting, and I ask, "What do you mean by socializing?"

"Too many times someone comes up with an idea like this. They create a form or procedure and shove it down everyone's throat. They don't consider others' perspectives, and as a result, nothing really changes."

She turns around abruptly in her chair to face her monitor as a signal this meeting is over, and with that, her compliment is finished as abruptly as any comment she makes.

It's that time of the week. The dreaded review meeting. I do my best to get everything together and take a deep breath, hoping we make some progress on breaking down all the conflicts we have been running into.

The first good sign is that people actually arrive on time. I arrive fifteen minutes before, and that last person to arrive from the core team we identified sits down at 12:59. Wow. So to honor their commitment, I start the meeting promptly at 1:00 p.m. I tee up the agenda we agreed to and everyone nods with approval. I also mention I would like to leave time to allow Kim to raise a topic for us to discuss something that impacts all of us. So I ask if we can leave forty-five minutes at the end of the meeting for that.

LaDonna, the head of engineering, speaks up and asks if she can have five minutes to talk about the meeting name. I'm shocked, since she is one of those quiet ones who only speaks when spoken to. Also, I appreciate her bringing up the meeting name. I forgot I suggested we consider a new name. "Weekly review meeting" does little to inspire or engage people. Even though it's only a name, changing it might give us new focus and also provide some excitement. I'm sensitive that even if we change the name, what happens in the meeting needs to be different too.

Since it's only five minutes, I ask the group if we should tackle that first. Plus, I'm curious what she has in mind. Everyone agrees.

She explains that our discussion last week got her thinking about what we do in this meeting. "Of course, my mind goes to problem solving, but I think it's bigger than that. We need to think ahead and find ways to get ahead of our customers' needs, and if possible, leapfrog our competitors. So instead of focusing on something boring like meetings, review, or something negative like problem solving, I came up with another word: breakthrough. What we need to do is find ways to break through problems, but also break through in finding better ways to do business."

I see lots of heads nodding, and LaDonna has a self-satisfied smile, not only for coming up with the word, but for stepping out of her comfort zone to speak up. Dom, our naysaying IT manager, tosses out one of his typical comments.

"We'll probably do more breaking than breaking through." He smiles because he is half teasing and knows he is playing to his stereotype. Several people throw wadded-up pieces of paper at him, and everyone, including Dom, chuckles. The group seems to be coming together.

I ask, "So what is the name, breakthrough review, breakthrough meeting?" Both of those words are probably taboo now since "review" and "meeting" are painted black from the previous name.

Dom says, "How about Breakthrough Forum?" Everyone does a double-take to see if he really made a positive contribution. More heads nod, and I think we have a first shot at it. I suggest we try it out for a week and see if it sticks.

We roll into the regular meeting agenda we agreed to at our last meeting. There is more structure, but there is still some chaos about whether we are talking about last week's orders, this week's orders, resources, or anything else.

I watch the discussions and keep them moving along to keep us on time. We seem to make better progress and make some key decisions that in the past would have been left open. I still see some people licking wounds from the battles and others who have sat back and not engaged. We still have some work to do, but for now, we're getting better.

As we wrap up the regular agenda items, I'm surprised we're ahead of schedule and glad we have time for Kim's topic on special orders. I was worried we wouldn't have time. I walk them through the TBT process I had reviewed with each person individually. I direct them toward the printed copies of the TBT template.

Before we begin, I walk through some guidance I created for these conversations to try to keep them on track. I explain the conversational approach I came up with by observing the manufacturing process, along with its three key parts: Identify, Explore, and Act.

"Kim, by using the TBT, is only providing the Identify part. By identifying, it doesn't mean Kim owns the solution, but she will lead the discussion and also take care of documenting what comes from the conversations."

I emphasize the importance of getting better understanding and clarity around these topics. "So it is up to us to ask questions and fully explore the topic." I suggest we focus on asking questions to get clarity and making sure we hear from everyone before we jump in with our own ideas or agendas.

"Lastly, we don't want to just talk about this topic, but find what action we might take. To that end, I am going to leave fifteen minutes at the end to get everyone's thoughts on where we can go from here." I pull out a stack of three-by-five cards, a suggestion from Carl, and put them on the table. When we're done, I'm going to ask each person to share at least one thing they think we can do based on our discussions. Kim will be the person who summarizes this and will lead us on anything we choose to do with this topic. That doesn't mean she owns it, just that she will own making sure we have a plan.

I pass out the TBT outline and Peter's suggestion that we keep it inside the guardrails by making sure we focus on the topic as Kim defines it and the ask she has of the group.

"So given that, I'm suggesting that Kim take about five minutes or less to tee up the topic. If we leave fifteen minutes at the end to hear from everyone, I figure we have about forty-five minutes for discussion to make sure we wrap up our meeting on time."

Everyone nods, and I think we're ready. It's hard to turn it over to Kim and see where it goes, not knowing what will happen. But between my conversations with Peter, Carolyn, and Kim while helping her prepare, I can trust the process.

She does a good job presenting the topic succinctly, and she does so in less than five minutes. I suggest we get any questions from people on the table first. The group tries to follow that approach, and some good questions come forth, but too many are really suggestions with a question mark. For example, "Have you thought of . . ." or "Don't you think . . ."

And like the toddler told not to grab the cookie, the group transitions to offering ideas after a relatively short period of time. They can't help themselves. Heck, I can't help myself either. I keep asking the group what questions we have to consider related to this topic. I let the conversations swirl around the room. I have no more control over the flow than I do over a raging river. The good news is that everyone is engaged and there are good ideas surging forward.

I watch the clock, and when we have about fifteen minutes left, I stop the discussion. "Just to make sure we end on time and we also get some good recommendations on what we can do next, I want to shift our thinking. Would each of you grab one of the three-by-five cards on the table and write down your answer to this question: 'Based on everything we have discussed so far, what thoughts would you recommend to Kim if we are to move forward?'"

IT CAN BE HARD TO HOLD BACK FROM OFFERING SUGGESTIONS, OPINIONS, AND IDEAS BEFORE UNDERSTANDING SOMETHING FULLY.

Jim, our head of logistics, jumps in and starts speaking before writing anything down. He is one of those hijackers in meetings. I politely stop him and ask him to write first. "We will hear from everyone, so don't worry. Let's give everyone a couple of minutes to capture their thoughts in writing. Even if you get done, can I ask that we sit quietly to give people time to finish their thoughts without interruption." I say this more as an instruction than a question.

Jim complies, and I look around the room and see heads down as people put serious thought to the question. I'm excited to see what they come up with.

I notice Bill, our controller, is writing extensively. It looks like he could write the Bible on a grain of sand. I'm glad we keep it to a three-by-five. But what's also interesting is the amount of thought and energy Bill is putting into this. He is one who rarely contributes to meetings. I always thought that given the choice, he would put on Harry Potter's invisibility cloak and disappear from the meetings. This is the most I have seen him appear to be engaged, and he hasn't even said anything yet. I can't to hear what he comes up with.

The silence is a little uncomfortable, but this seems to have broken scrum we generally have in meetings where everyone piles on all at once. Once I see the group is done, I suggest we go around rapid-fire and hear from everyone. Rapid-fire is bit of wisdom Carolyn gave me. She suggested that by calling it rapid-fire, you're telling the group to be quick and succinct. Even though they only have a three-by-five card to write on, I'm sure some people would be likely to use that to deliver a lengthy homily.

I ask the group to not interrupt the person speaking nor add on to what they say, just listen. I let them know if they have something to add, we will come back and open up the floor for anything else that might be spurred from any of the feedback. "In this way, we hear from everyone, and everyone has an equal chance to share uninterrupted."

The group nods. I ask Bill to go first because I'm dying to hear what might be cooped up in his head as the quiet one in the group.

"Oh yeah," I add one more piece of guidance, "I find round robin to be fairly dry." I'm referring to the process where you go around the table one by one. "I would like to suggest that we mix things up and bounce around the room. Bill, since you are going first, I would ask you to pick who goes next. The only caveat is that you cannot pick someone sitting next to you. Then we will repeat that until we hear from everyone."

Bill summarizes the three bullets he wrote on his three-by-five card in his usual curt and methodical mannerism. He suggests we first put together a small team to handle all current and future special orders. "We need to get a handle on these quickly. Then I suggest we put together a separate team to recommend how we handle special orders in the future. Give them a couple of weeks to come back to this group with some initial recommendation. Lastly, once we have reviewed and agreed as a team, we schedule a time with senior management to review and approve what the team recommends."

I'm glad we started with Bill, because he set the pace and showed how to deliver rapid-fire. I'm pleased with how the process is going.

As a matter of fact, I notice the energy in the room is very different, and we get some great insights from the group. Some people offer similar ideas, but then share some additions or refinements to thoughts that were already expressed. For example, Sally also suggests a team for special orders, but she suggests calling them a SWAT team. Jim suggests we might have different types of special orders and we might need to create classifications or categories of special orders. Some of the feedback doesn't involve a specific recommendation, but offers insights like ways special orders are costing us both money and customers. Overall, we make significant progress.

I ask Kim to share what jumped out at her and what her initial thoughts are based on the feedback. She does a good job synthesizing the feedback and also thanks the group for giving her, and all of us, some great input to work on. She offers to summarize the feedback and come back next week with a more concise set of recommendations for the group to review.

Lots of heads nod; there's lots of energy and even some smiles. By way of wrap-up, I say, "This type of discussion has been hard for us. Too often it turns into a war of blame with everyone lobbing bombshells at each other. I'm impressed how we actually came together, worked on an issue causing serious conflicts, and walked away with some progress made. We didn't solve it entirely, but I think that would have been unrealistic. Thanks to Kim, she named the gap we have, and as a group, we made progress closing the gap. Thank you."

The nice thing with the three-by-five cards is that we have a written record of what was shared. I'm sure I didn't understand the full essence of what people were saying, so I make a mental note to go through the note cards with Kim.

I also like that it made people commit to something. There are people, who will remain nameless (Dom from IT), who love to complain and never commit to any position. This gives them cover anytime something goes wrong. Now he has to put a stake in the group and make some kind of stand.

"As we adjourn our meeting, can I ask each of you to write your name on the three-by-five card and pass it to Kim? This will help her to remember what you shared and also to follow up with you if something isn't clear."

I adjourn the meeting and glance at the clock, seeing that we are five minutes early. Joanne sees me eye the clock as she walks out and offers a quick "Nice job" with a hint of a smile. Wow, that, for her, is as effusive as she gets, and I accept the compliment with a thank-you. I don't know if she heard it because she was halfway over the threshold of the doorway as she said it.

For a change, I'm not in the conference room well into the evening after our weekly review meeting, I mean Breakthrough Forum. I am in my office, tending to the day's business. It isn't too late, but it is dark outside, as winter is still prominent this time of year. Because of the darkness, my office window becomes a mirror. I'm faced away from the door, but I see Carolyn's reflection in the window as she passes by in the hallway. I give a quick shout to see if she has a minute, to which she obliges. Without needing an invitation, she grabs a seat at my discussion table, and without asking, I grab a bottled water from my fridge and toss it to her.

"I didn't want to interrupt you, but I'm dying to hear how the meeting went."

I give her a fairly detailed overview of everything. I thank her for her ideas and input. "Overall, I think we made great progress turning conflict into something actionable. I am struggling with one thing, though."

"What's that?"

"Even though the group tried to ask questions first, there was the natural momentum that drove people to jump in and offer suggestions. Sometimes it's subtle, like questions that were really suggestions in sheep's clothing. Others were just overt suggestions. Although I think it's good to get ideas out, I found people started down that path well before we really understood 'the gap' causing the conflict." I confess my own sin in wanting to do the same thing.

"It makes sense, though," she says. "It's what our brain is hardwired to do. If it sees a problem, it wants to solve it." I nod as she continues. "Plus, no one wants to see someone struggle, so when we see someone with a problem, we want to help them out of the situation."

"But we know that old saying about giving someone a fish versus teaching them to fish," I say. "So we know it's better to help people figure it out. What is the antidote to this fatal flaw?"

"Well, I wouldn't throw the baby out with the bathwater. There are clearly times our ability to offer advice and suggestions is a useful skill. However, like any skill that is overused, it can become a weakness. We need to train ourselves out of this habit."

"But how?" I ask.

"I'm not sure what will work for your group. What do you think?"

I'm thinking more about myself than how to fix others. Most change starts with ourselves, and we can model good leadership for others.

I pull out one of the blank three-by-five cards left over from the meeting and write: "Ask first, listen second." That will be an important step for me.

Carolyn asks me to explain. "I think I should work on myself first. Plus, each person might have a different idea of what to do for themselves. Who am I to say what anyone should be trying to do?"

"If you ask first, listen second, what comes after that?" she asks with a sly smile.

"I think that should be a loop. If I ask first and listen second, I might need to loop back and ask again and listen again to make sure I understand," I reply with my own sly smile.

"So where does this end?" she teases me further.

"I guess that if I asked, listened, and understood, maybe then the door should be open to me speaking at that point."

I update my card so that it now reads: "Ask first, listen second, speak last."

She walks over to my desk and takes one of my picture holders that has an alligator clip on a wire and asks if she can borrow it for a moment.

"Sure," I say, curious where this is going.

She removes the picture, brings it back to the table, and puts my three-by-five card in the clip and points the side with my writing toward me.

"I think that's a great start. Let me know how it goes? I hate to run, but I have some ground to cover. Talk to you soon." I hear her whistling "Whistle While You Work" as she makes her way down the hallway.

ASK FIRST, LISTEN SECOND, SPEAK LAST.

I think, *I should whistle while I get the hell out of here for the day.* I start whistling a chipper tune as I grab my coat and head for the door. It has been a good day.

Carl calls in the early evening just as I sit down to my evening snack. It's a snack because I still don't have the hang of cooking for one. So my evening is usually a plate of things I can scrounge from the kitchen to give me some sustenance. Tonight it is some cheese, carrots, celery, and hummus.

I settle into my chair and fill Carl in on the meeting. I share with him the successes and the trials. "Overall, I think we made some good progress closing some gaps in the conflicts we've been having. For example, we have more agreement on the orders and how they need to be prioritized. We had far fewer arguments, bombshells, and personal attacks. We seem to be making progress on making decisions. I think part of it is because they feel ownership since the senior leaders aren't in the room to defer to on every little matter."

I share with him the topic Kim raised around special orders and how she did a great job framing it for everyone. "We actually got to see it was two things. First, how we're handling them today, but also that we need to put something in place to handle them going forward."

"What did they come up with?"

"They came up with some good ideas." I explain the process of writing feedback on the cards, then add, "And Kim is going to summarize them for the next meeting to review and start on some strategies to solve both challenges."

"So what's next for this group?"

I shared with him the challenges of people wanting to jump in with solutions and the need for everyone to ask better questions. "Not just the team, but I found it challenging." I even shared with him my note card—"Ask first, listen second, speak last"—I created from my conversation with Carolyn.

"That sounds like a simple but powerful thing to do," he affirms.

"I'm going to bring it to the next meeting and keep it in front of me."

"Great idea," he says. "I just had a flash about your idea to create principles of engagement for the team. Maybe this could be the start of that. You just defined a principle for you . . ."

". . . and why not invite them to do the same for themselves," I finish his sentence.

We finish up our call with some non-work-related things. I still have this feeling of subtext to his calls, but I can't put my finger on it and he doesn't say anything. Although there's still a comfort in thinking about going back to my old job, if asked, I also am starting to gain my sea legs at my current job.

We bid good evening and end our call. Time to finish my grazing and get ready for bed.

Chapter 6

Learning to Explore

Peter shows up at my door early the next morning, again with a fresh coffee in hand. I joke to myself, *I don't care if he is bribing me, if he keeps showing up with coffee he can have whatever he wants next time he asks.*

He asks about the meeting, and for the third time in less than twenty-four hours I walk someone through the meeting progress. I actually appreciate doing so, because it gives me time to reflect on the meeting and reinforce the things we did well, plus affirm the next steps. It's also helpful to know I have people in my corner.

I update him on the success of the regular meeting agenda and how the team is taking ownership of making the day-to-day decisions. He says, "Steve Jobs would be proud."

I look at him with shock as he reiterates the exact same Steve Jobs' quote I had considered when I was forming the meeting: "It doesn't make sense to hire smart people and tell them what to do; we hire smart people so they can tell us what to do."

I nod with a sense of self-appreciation. "You're letting the smart people make the decisions. As a matter of fact, I'm reminded of something an old mentor told me. He used to say, 'Most innovation in an organization comes from the front line.' Too many times we look up in the organization for the senior people to solve big problems, but they don't have the firsthand experience. We need to ask the people on the front line."

> **LET SMART PEOPLE MAKE THE DECISIONS. MOST INNOVATION COMES FROM THE FRONT LINE.**

This serves as a good pivot point to update him on the topic-briefing framework he helped me with. I pull out the document I created and share with him how I reviewed it with the team and actually helped Kim tee up an important topic in our meeting. I explain how she used this approach to talk about the special request issues we are facing. He nods in a gratified agreement.

Even though I think we made great progress, I share with him the struggle with myself, and the rest of the team, asking good questions.

"I think we all know we need to do a better job asking questions, but it's just so damn easy to jump to our default setting of telling versus asking. But also, I feel like we don't know what to ask. For example, what would I even ask if I wanted to ask more questions?"

Peter is a great listener, which makes it easy for me to share and think it through. I realize part of the power of great questions is not in the question itself, but in the silence after the question. That silence gives the other person time to think, just like Peter is doing right now.

"I notice when you ask a question, you let it reverberate, like when a bell rings. You're letting the quiet work, and the question keeps reverberating in my brain," I say with a smile of thanks.

He says, "Sometimes the best part of the question isn't the question, it's what the person does with it in her head."

> **ASKING GOOD QUESTIONS IS LIKE PULLING A THREAD.**

Peter continues to expand our conversation. "I agree, it can be hard to know what to ask. I think of asking questions like pulling a thread. You start with a question, the answer to which reveals the next question you might ask. And you keep pulling the thread. But there are also multiple threads you might pull."

The confusion on my face tells him he just threw me for a loop with that little ditty. "What do you mean multiple threads?"

"When I go into a client meeting or negotiation, there are types of questions I plan to ask. For example, I might have questions about the situation they are facing, challenges they are trying to address, or the impact to the business. It is also true for doctors in triage; there are types of questions they are going to ask regardless of the illness or injury, like current medications, vital signs, or symptoms. I wonder if in your setting there might be types of questions you might ask that could tell you what threads to pull. Rather than thinking about what question to ask, think about threads."

He looks at my whiteboard as he gets up to leave. He points to my definition and says, "It seems you have done a good job identifying the gap, and it sounds like you're ready to focus on exploring the gap to get a better understanding."

I notice he has used both my definition and the conversational process language (Identify and Explore).

"Thank you, Peter," I say as he heads out of my office.

"Don't mention it." But I still have that feeling this will be coming back as a favor he will ask of me at some future date.

I don't want to lose the momentum of the thought process Peter just spurred. Figuring out how to explore, or ask better questions, is the next key for me and our team. If we want to use conflict to increase our understanding, as we stated in our definition, we need to provide ways to do so.

I pick up the phone and make a few calls to get some other brains working on this. Thirty minutes later, I have five people sitting around the table in the small conference room. There is no rocket science behind who is in attendance; it was who was available. I have Kim, my customer service supervisor; LaDonna, the head of engineering; Sally, the sales operations supervisor; Bill, the controller; and yes, even Dom, our naysaying head of IT.

I've written the definition of conflict on the whiteboard . . .

CONFLICT: A GAP BETWEEN WHAT WE EXPECT AND WHAT WE EXPERIENCE THAT LEADS TO DEEPER UNDERSTANDING AND BETTER RESULTS.

. . . as well as the conversation process we have identified using the manufacturing process as a model (Identify, Explore, and Act).

I start sharing with them my hope that we can find a way, an approach, if you will, to ask better questions in our team meeting. I start by reviewing the definition and our conversational process as a foundation. I point to the middle of our definition where it says "create deeper understanding" and suggest that when we are in conflict, we fail to see the whole picture. I then point to the middle of our conversational process and continue: "This part of our definition and our need to explore both suggest we need to ask better questions." I explain Peter's comment about pulling the threads and thinking about the types of questions we might ask.

"What I would like to do in the next forty-five minutes is get some initial thoughts on types of questions we might be asking and see if we can organize it in a way that helps our group."

I realize that without even planning it, I just used our TBT framework to tee up the topic. I named it succinctly, gave some background, and stated a clear and reasonable ask. *Hey, this really works,* I say to myself. I even have a stack of three-by-five cards on the table to help with the wrap-up.

After I open up the discussion, things get messy, but a good messy. Lots of different perspectives are being shared. No one is discounting what someone says or talking over others. I'm doing my best to capture everything coming out on the whiteboard. The whiteboard is as messy as the conversation, but again, the good kind of messy.

We start to see some themes come up.

LaDonna, the consummate engineer, says, "I just want the facts. I see lots of fact-type questions, like what's happening, how long, who else is involved. It reminds me of a professor who used to say, 'Look for the Five Ws: who, what, when, where, and how.'"

Dom says jokingly, "Looks like your engineering professor missed the spelling class," referring to the fact that "how" actually starts with an H, not a W.

Everyone chuckles, and LaDonna clarifies that he said the last letter of how is a W, which consummates the Five Ws.

Bill says, "What about the why questions we have up there, like why are we focusing on this, why is this important?"

LaDonna continues. "That's a good question. First, he would say that the Five Ws are the data questions, so collect the data. Should we combine the why questions with the Five Ws and make it six?"

There is a silence as she, and the rest of the group, ponder this. She continues, "As I look at the why questions, they seem different than data."

Dom chimes in, "The why questions seem like questions about meaning; it's more about what something means or what its purpose is."

I've gone over to another whiteboard and written "Data questions," and then underneath, "Five Ws: who, what, when, where, how."

I write next to it "Why," and underneath I write, "Meaning/purpose," and a couple of prompting questions like, "Why is this important to talk about? How does this relate to our goals/purpose? Why do we care about this?"

Continuing to identify categories of questions to better explore, Bill, our company controller, jumps in saying that when he looks at a situation, he wants to know the risks. "There are lots of questions up there related to risks. For example, I want to know how it might impact the budget, or present risks to other funded projects. Should Risk be a category?"

Dom from IT builds on that by talking about the risk-assessment methods they use in IT anytime they have a project. "Our boss makes us think through a variety of risks and has a framework we use. It includes things like scope risk, platform risks, financial risks, resource risks, risks due to changes in technology, and a whole bunch more. We don't have to address all of them, but we need to be prepared to identify any that might relate to our project."

That explains why Dom is considered our naysayer; he is forced to look at risks. I realize many times people see him as an obstructionist, when in actuality he's just pointing out risks. There are people and functions that are more disciplined to think about risk, like IT, but also finance, quality control, and engineering. Instead of seeing them as cynical or pessimistic, we should welcome these types' contributions since they help us to see risks.

Sally interrupts my mental sidebar. "I see risk a little differently. My father gave me some of that sage advice, you know the kind. We don't really listen to or understand our parents at the time, but then later we realize they are much wiser than we give them credit for. He said when you feel afraid, fear is pointing to some kind of risk. He said our whole life is spent managing risks, and it shows up in the form of fear. So when we feel that fear, put a name to it and see it as a risk. For example, when I get a new assignment, I might be afraid I won't have enough time to finish it. Then he would say you can start thinking about what to do with that risk. So rather than sit in fear, he said to think of what choices I have." She continues. "He said you have one of four choices when you see a risk, and he gave me the acronym AACT as a way to think about managing those choices: avoid it, accept the risk, control it, or transfer it."

I've created a new column of things to explore: Risk. I write a few prompts underneath: "What are we afraid of," "What could come back to bite us," and "What types of risk we need to consider." I even add Sally's father's AACT. That's worth exploring further.

LaDonna sees something in my eyes and asks, "Angela, you seem like you have something to say and you aren't saying it."

She got me. "There is something I'm thinking about, but I'm not sure how to say it."

"Go ahead, just toss it out and let's see what you're thinking."

I sit down in a chair instead of standing at the whiteboard. "I've noticed we have too many times when we blame other people. Sometimes it's very direct and we attack someone in the meeting. Other times it's more subtle. We may not say the person's name, but everyone knows who's being attacked. Also, there are times when it may not be a person, it could be a whole department."

Everyone is paying close attention, and I can't tell if they're in agreement or not. I continue anyway. "Let's take an example. Last week, I was talking with my team about a customer problem. There were too many comments putting the blame on IT." Dom sits forward, ready to get defensive. "However, it's too easy to blame other people. As a matter of fact, blaming others can be a way of keeping negative attention away from ourselves. I have to admit that it was comfortable for me to let IT take the blame because it kept customer support out of hot water. But if we take the time to think about it, the problem may not reside with a specific programmer, or even IT overall." Dom sits back for the moment.

"It's easy to blame others, and it's hard to look at ourselves. Our default is to find that person who's going to die here today, which makes everyone defensive. The goal is to either launch a preemptive strike on others or dodge the bullets when they're flying."

Sally says, "But no one is likely to step up and say, 'Hey, it was my fault.'"

I continue. "And why would anyone else ever take responsibility if something goes wrong, if others aren't willing to do the same thing?"

I refer to the whiteboard, where the definition of conflict as a gap is written prominently. "That's why thinking about conflict as a gap can help us. Instead of blaming others, we can look at the gap, and it helps to depersonalize the situation."

LaDonna jumps in. "It's what my mentor used to call 'the sin of externalization.'" That grabbed everyone's attention, their expressions seeming to say, What the heck does that mean?

LaDonna continues. "My mentor would say our natural inclination is to look outside of ourselves when there is a problem, to lay blame at the feet of others. She told me we need to do a better job looking inward first. To ask ourselves, 'In what way may we have contributed?' It's like that old saying, when you're pointing at someone else, you have three fingers pointing back at you."

She says, "May I?" as she grabs the marker and adds another column to our questions on the whiteboard: Internal reflection. She adds a couple of bullets under that: "Is there any way I may have contributed? Is my DNA on the crime scene? What could I have done differently to avoid this situation? What might others say about how I might have contributed?"

I shift in my seat as she goes through these questions, and I see the rest of the group doing the same.

Dom asks in his best defensive tone that emanates from years of people blaming IT for every little problem: "What if I didn't contribute to the problem?"

She underlines the word "may" and says, "It's not about laying blame on ourselves or getting others to do the same. It's about exploring where we might have a piece of the situation we're facing."

Dom continues to challenge the idea. "Well, I'll be darned if I'm going to take responsibility when others don't do the same."

"I get it," LaDonna says. "This is hard to ask, and hard to do. Especially when we're hardwired to find blame in others. But this is just one set of questions we can explore." She emphasizes the word "explore" because that is what we are working on. "It can give us pause to look inward, both as individuals and as teams."

Sally jumps in and says, "This could be one way to get us out of the blame game. In the situation Angela mentioned where we were blaming IT for a customer problem, we ended up having a very healthy discussion about how we had helped create the problem. And that's where we needed to start."

Bill jumps in, as he has been quiet. He calls this stuff "touchy feely," and it's clearly not his comfort zone. "So why haven't we talked about exploring the impact on the business? After all, any conversation we have should relate to how it impacts the business. That's why we show up here every day, to manage a business."

LaDonna still has the marker and writes another column that reads, "Business Impact." I'm glad to see LaDonna taking the lead with the discussion so it isn't just me. "Does that capture it, Bill?" she asks as confirmation. He nods. She continues, "So what would be under this if we were to explore the business impact?"

Sally pipes in for Bill. "Well, Bill always tells me that whatever we do impacts revenue, cost, or cash." She smiles at Bill to show she has been paying attention.

Bill smiles back and says, "That captures it." He looks proud that Sally seems to care about the financial part of the business.

I pipe in. "We have five good categories to explore and some suggestions under each one on questions to consider. What do you all think?"

After some idle rambling, it seems we have a fairly complete outline. I say to the group, "I came into this hoping to find some ways to do a better job exploring topics more effectively as a team. Let's wrap up with a question to make sure we get your final thoughts. Given everything we discussed, what do you think is the most powerful step or steps we can take now? Why don't we each grab a card to write down our best thinking around that question?"

This time we don't have to discuss how the process works. Everyone grabs a card and gets writing. We use the same rapid-fire approach as before, and in less than five minutes I have some great suggestions.

"I think we have a good start to providing a framework. I'll summarize this and send it back out to everyone so you can add any thoughts that occur to you later. Since several people suggested we engage the rest of the team with this framework, are you okay with sharing this at this week's meeting?"

No objections, so it's safe to assume everyone is in alignment.

"So who should review this with the team?" I ask, knowing they all assume it will be me. I'm glad to see LaDonna volunteer. She made some solid contributions to the discussion when it isn't natural for her to speak up. I respect that she has stepped out of her comfort zone. I check the clock, and we're done right on time. I adjourn the group with a sense of self-satisfaction.

First thing the next morning, Peter is back in my office. He walks in and looks over my desk to see what I'm writing as he sets a fresh coffee down next to the large sheet of paper where I've been busy scribing yesterday's notes. Noticing the word "Explore" is prominently written on the top of the sheet, he says, "Looks like you've made quite a bit of progress on exploring. What do you have there?"

Last night, I doodled an Explore loop to go inside of my conversation loop. It's a loop within a loop, and it shows each of the five types of Explore questions we came up with. I give Peter examples for each, and he gives me that satisfied nod. "I'm impressed." I share with him that the team did a great job of really fleshing it out.

"I'm going to review it with the team at this week's meeting, get any additional input and see if we can start putting it into practice. I'm drawing up this poster so we can hang it in the room."

"Do you think we missed anything?" I ask.

He looks at it for a few minutes, not saying anything. He offers a couple of additional prompts we can use in the different categories. "I wouldn't change the categories, I think what you all came up with is pretty comprehensive."

He continues, "I think this is something we can use throughout the company. Our ability to ask better questions is central to our company, just like 'better understanding' is central in your definition of conflict and exploring is central to your IdEA Model. Everything revolves around getting curious."

I like his use of the word curious, because just asking questions alone isn't enough. Questions need to be backed up by a sincere interest in understanding, in listening, and in learning. "I notice the team, and quite honestly myself, tends to be more comfortable making statements than asking questions."

"I know what you mean," Peter says. "Someone once told me our curiosity is at its highest from the time we are born until we are around five years old. And for many, it declines over time, some faster than others." He finishes with that charmer smile, like he's going to name people who have depleted all of their curiosity.

"So how can we change that ratio?" I ask. At that moment, an equation appears in my mind's eye. I pull out a three-by-five card and write, "Curiosity = Questions Asked/Statements Made."

$$Curiosity = \frac{Questions\ Asked}{Statements\ Made}$$

Peter turns his head sideways so he can read what I wrote. "Interesting, what does that mean?"

I explain my thinking around getting people to ask more questions versus making statements. A word suddenly comes to mind: "Quotient," I say out loud.

Peter says, "That word, quotient, resonates for me like when it's used in the IQ intelligence test or EQ to assess emotional intelligence. Maybe we can use a curiosity quotient as a way to measure our curiosity."

So I write it next to the word "curiosity" so it now reads, "Curiosity Quotient = Questions Asked/Statements Made."

$$\text{Curiosity Quotient} = \left(\frac{\textit{Questions Asked}}{\textit{Statements Made}} \right)$$

Peter adds, "I like it. But what's that unsettled look you have?"

"I think this captures it, but it's missing one thing. I remember working with someone who asked lots of questions, so he would have a high CQ. However, the way he came across wasn't the best. He would pepper you with questions to the point you thought you were being interrogated. The group used to call meetings with him 'Wally Waterboarding.'"

"It seems the equation needs balance. It doesn't sound like you have to have all questions and no statements to have a good CQ," Peter says.

I build on that statement. "There needs to be give and take, that the person asking questions needs to contribute as well. If you just ask questions, it can make people defensive. But there was more to it: Wally's questions always had an undertone, like he wanted to look like he was smarter than you, or sometimes it felt like his questions were a 'gotcha.' It was like a conversation with him was a competition."

"So what's missing from the equation?" Peter asks.

We stare at it for a while. When I finally speak I say, "There needs to be a genuine interest." I look up at the definition of conflict on the whiteboard. "Which ties into our definition that says we use conflict to create deeper understanding, for everyone. Without that, this means nothing. As a matter of fact, I used to work with someone who used to say, 'I'm just curious' when he was in this type of conversation. And he really was just curious. It was a very disarming statement and engendered people to share."

"So how do you think that fits in the equation?" Peter asks.

I start to think as I talk. "I think mutual understanding is the variable we need to add, and my first thought is that it's a multiplier. That we multiply the equation by the desire for mutual understanding. But I think the desire for mutual understanding is so important it's stronger than just a multiplier, it's . . ."

And Peter and I finish the sentence together, "Exponential."

I finish my equation by putting a bracket around the equation and write, "Mutual Understanding," so it now reads:

$$Curiosity\ Quotient = \left(\frac{Questions\ Asked}{Statements\ Made} \right)^{Mutual\ Understanding}$$

"Nice work," he says as he gathers his coffee to head out the door. Still having that feeling that he's going to ask for something, I decide to pop the question on him. "Before you go, is there anything I can do for you, Peter?"

"You just did. I definitely learned something here today. Thank you for letting me be part of your thinking." And with that, he's off to whatever is next in his day for him.

I take the equation I wrote on the three-by-five card and I tape it on the whiteboard next to "Explore" in the IdEA framework. Having finished up with Peter, I have just enough time to forage for some more coffee before I need to get ready for my one-on-one with Kim, my supervisor.

When I come back to my office, Kim is there ready for our meeting. She's staring at the whiteboard, focused on the three-by-five card with the CQ equation. She has her journal open and is writing in it.

"Hi Kim," I greet her as I pay it forward for the coffees Peter has been bringing me. I bring Kim her favorite morning beverage, Diet Coke.

"Thank you." She smiles as she takes her first gulp. "I was just reviewing your handiwork and honestly reviewing the IdEA framework so we can use that approach in our one-on-one. I have a couple of items I've identified and even outlined using the TBT."

"I noticed your equation here." She points to the three-by-five card on the whiteboard. "I'm not sure where it came from, but I get it immediately without any explanation. That's pretty slick. It ties into the discussion we had the other day trying to come up with better ways to explore topics. I wrote it in my journal, if you don't mind me borrowing it."

"It's yours, take it for a few laps around the office," I say. "Drive it like you stole it."

She chuckles. "Quite honestly, I've been thinking about this whole 'Explore' thing since our meeting yesterday. I realize how often I don't ask questions. I know I need to do a better job. But I never know what to ask. I've been thinking about the types of questions we came up with, and it's very helpful." She continues, "As a matter of fact, as I prepared for our meeting today, I tried to think of the types of questions we raised so I could think through them."

"But . . ." I say, sensing she ran into a roadblock.

"I got caught up in my own mind and got stuck. I think I thought through this better than I would have otherwise, but I'm not sure I've fully explored this. I realize that's where I need your help. Too many times I've been coming to these one-on-ones expecting you to give me the answers or impart some knowledge about my challenges. What I think I really need is time with you to puzzle through this, to have you ask me questions I haven't thought about yet."

Wow, I think to myself, *I too have been thinking about our one-on-ones the wrong way.* She just titled my brain with that. Time to reset. I pull out the large sheet of paper where I've been capturing our notes on the different Explore topics and questions. "Let's take this out for a test drive. If you don't mind, I will keep this with us as a reminder for me to help you puzzle through our topics." I also share that I would like to test out our curiosity quotient. "When we're done, I would like your thoughts on how I did using the equation."

> **HOW CAN YOU HELP OTHERS PUZZLE THROUGH THE QUESTIONS THEY HAVEN'T THOUGHT OF YET?**

"Agreed," she says, and with that, we jump into the first topic.

As we're talking, I realize how bumpy this feels. I'm conscious of what I'm asking and thinking about what I might not be asking. I also keep looking at the Explore categories and realize I want to use this in a linear way. For example, exhaust all of the 5W or data questions before going to the next category. What I find is that we bounce around a bit. We talk about risk, and next we talk about business impact, then we go back to data questions. It feels a bit disheveled.

I am also very conscious every time I make some type of statement. I'm wondering if I should be asking more questions and if, by introducing my thoughts, I'm taking over her topic and leading her down a path I want her to go, versus what might be the right path for her. I have no idea what the right balance of questions to statements is.

When we get done, Kim and I talk about how it went. I'm glad to hear that although she sensed some of my discomfort, she thought process was not that bumpy. Maybe it's more in my head.

"What I appreciated is that you let the conversation go where it needed to go," Kim says. "I didn't feel like you were steering me or trying to get me to follow some formula. It felt like you followed up with questions related to what I shared. I think if you had gone from category to category, it would have seemed artificial and stilted. It felt messy to me too at times, and that can be frustrating, but I found that through the messiness, I actually ended up with better understanding and order to my thoughts."

She did notice there were times when I jumped in with my thoughts or recommendations prematurely. "It didn't bother me, and many times what you shared spurred some of my thinking. I thought it helped because you would say something and then let me decide if I wanted to pursue it further."

She wraps up by saying, "Overall, if we look at our CQ, it seems like a much better balance than many of the conversations we have at work. I did think you came across as curious and interested. That trumps any question you might ask. It felt like this was a place to really puzzle through things. As long as we both sense a balance, I think we're getting better."

After we wrap up our one-on-one and Kim has left, I sit with my thoughts and reflect on the process we just experienced together. I think there are some important points to remember, and I capture them in my notebook. I write these down to make sure I share them with others as we try out our framework:

✔ Let the conversation go where it needs to go; don't get too caught up in following a process.

✔ It's okay to jump from questions in one category to questions in another. It should not be stilted.

✔ Conversations are messy, and it's okay to let them be messy. Out of chaos comes order.

✔ CQ is about balance. Do you have the right balance

of questions and statements? Ask the other person if they think you have the right balance.

✓ Offering an idea or an observation can help the other person. They can decide if they want to pursue that thought, not as something forced upon them.

✓ Genuine interest trumps any questions or methods we may use.

I arrive early the next morning, long before anyone else, to get a head start on the day. I'm sitting in my office reviewing some paperwork when a shadow passing my door startles me. I look up to see Carolyn passing by. What is she doing here in the morning? Does this woman live here?

I shout out, "Hey there, how are you?" to see if she will stop back to chat. I haven't seen her in a few days, and I miss our conversations. The shadow returns and fills my doorway.

"What are you doing here so early the morning?" I ask.

"I was going to ask you the same thing. I thought you worked the late shift." She smiles. "I come early some days to check on inventories and supplies."

"Do you have some time to sit and chat?"

"Sure," she says as she grabs a seat at the guest table.

I walk her through our latest developments. The Explore part of the IdEA framework, the prompting questions, the CQ equation, my experience using this with Kim, even the notes I wrote as reminders about how to approach it better. She listens intently, asking questions to help me get clearer and offering some thoughts on the process.

"It seems you and the team have done some great work here. What's next?" she asks.

I look up at the IdEA framework and say, "I think we're ready to tackle the Action in our framework. That seems like it should be pretty easy. So why doesn't it feel that way?"

"What do you mean?'

"Well, it seems that for all of our good intentions and great ideas, too many times the likely outcome of our action plans is inaction. Things just don't get done."

Carolyn laughs. "It's like my great plan to lose that extra few pounds. It should be easy. I tell myself it is easy, eat less and exercise more, but I never seem to get there."

I think to myself, *What's missing, then?* "Like all of our grand designs to lose weight and how simple it should be, we don't really flesh it out enough to be clear about the action. I tell myself the same things and stumble too."

"So what's missing?" she asks, as much for herself as for me.

"We don't put enough detail behind it. For example, eat less of what or what kind of exercise and how often." I look at the Explore questions and notice our Five Ws can help (who, what, when, where, and how). "We should ask more questions when we define an action so it's clearer."

She says, "It's reminds me of a quote by Napoleon Hill, who said, 'What the mind can conceive and believe it can achieve.'"

"We don't get enough clarity on the outcomes we conceive." I make a note to myself to make sure we clearly define our actions and the Five Ws. "It still feels like we're missing something, though."

"What do you think is missing?" she asks.

"Well, for example, I say I'll get up early and go to the gym to exercise before work, because at the end of the day I'm too tired. Unfortunately, when I wake up, I start thinking about everything I need to do and head straight to the office."

"Sounds to me like you haven't thought about the risks to your plan," she says, looking at the Explore questions.

"That only reinforces how important it is to discuss risks in the Explore questions."

"Yes, *and*," she says, emphasizing the word, "*and* . . . we need to look for the things that are going to get in the way of an action we define. For example, I have the same problem you do. I don't go in the mornings because that is not a motivating time for me." I find it hard to believe this woman is ever not loaded with energy and motivated. She continues. "So either I need to find a better time or something that will get me over the hump of my morning motivation."

I look at the Explore categories and the "why" questions. "Hmm, if we have really taken the time to help the person understand their why and if it's big enough, it should motivate the person to achieve that. *And*," I say, emphasizing the word like she did, "if that doesn't work for them, they can identify an alternative before the plan falls flat on its face. I might like to get up early to exercise, but if the other person doesn't, we have a problem."

She continues, "And what if they don't like the gym? How motivated are they going to be to actually drag their butt out of bed to go there? That's why I cycle. It's an activity I truly enjoy; it's freeing. So I'm motivated to do that."

"That's why we come up with these grand ideas and they don't get done. We never address underlying motivations," I say as the lightbulb in my mind shines on this idea.

She adds, "*And*, I think too many times we name the action for people and they don't own it. We tell them how to lose weight instead of them defining how they're going to do it. I'm thinking about an old negotiating rule that says, 'The first person to name price loses.' That's why when you buy a car, the salesperson won't give you an exact price. I think the same thing happens when we're coming up with action plans. Not that it's a win/lose, but it seems that when a person names the action specifically, they're more likely to own it. I find I get more commitment, motivation, and ultimately results when I let my people pick the action. When I name it, I own it, and they're only partially committed and thus less likely to achieve a result."

I'm writing fast and furious in my notebook. "So we make sure that actions are defined in as much detail as possible, that there's a strong enough *why* from our Explore questions to motivate the action and give them the opportunity to name what they're willing to commit to." I continue. "Makes sense, but what if I have to tell them what they should do, or they pick the wrong idea, something that isn't possible?"

Carolyn sits there, letting me come up with my own thoughts around this.

"I guess it's a judgment call, isn't it?" I say as she nods. "Clearly there is a time we need to offer direction. I guess my question for myself is 'Is this the moment I need to tell them versus letting them figure it out?' And if they're going to drive the freight train over the cliff, I might need to put on the brakes."

She adds, "I never worry about my ability to tell people what to do. I can do that in spades. So this reminds me that I need to leave the door open more often for them to name the outcome they are willing to commit to."

I share with her the comment Dom made in one our first meetings about needing more resources. "So using his example, what if they say the action is to get more resources when we darn well know we have a pig's chance of flying in getting those resources?"

We both ponder that one for a minute. Carolyn speaks first. "It reminds me of a boss who would say, 'Stress is not about workload, it's about control.' I think of that often because too many times I focus on the things I can't control."

Picking up where she left off, I continue, "So we need to focus our action on where and in what ways we have control."

> **STRESS IS NOT ABOUT WORKLOAD, IT'S ABOUT CONTROL. FOCUS THE ACTION WHERE YOU HAVE CONTROL.**

"So what would you say to Dom in that situation?"

"Hmm, I guess I would start by saying, 'For the sake of discussion, let's agree we don't have the ability to get more resources right now. Where do you think we have control?'" I say, feeling somewhat satisfied.

"Okay," I continue, "that makes sense. But I also notice another challenge we run into when planning. We come up with this huge list of actions, overwhelming I would say, and none of them happen."

Carolyn looks thoughtful, then grabs a marker and starts writing on the whiteboard. When she is done, she reads aloud what she has written: "What is the most powerful step you can take right now?" She puts the marker down. "It seems you have a good framework to Identify and Explore. Now you've added Action. I look forward to seeing where you go with this."

As she bounds out of the office with her usual cheery goodbye, I'm left with that question staring at me. Did she ask that of me? I start pondering all of the things I can do with this framework, and actions run through my head like the cash register receipt from my last trip to the grocery. I know if I start with that list, I won't get anywhere. It's overwhelming.

There's something in the words that reverberates in me like a bell that has recently chimed. I go to the whiteboard and underline a few words that leap off the board, shouting for my attention. The first are "most powerful." It jumps at me because it immediately focused my mind on a few key things I can do, the most powerful things, those things that can have the greatest impact. I also underline "right now." I feel optimistic now that I have a couple of key actions in my head that will allow me to start putting this new framework in place. But the words "right now" force me to take a step. Even a small step is progress.

Before I put the marker down, I underline "you." Too many times we have the action items that say, "We need to . . ." But I can never figure out who "we" is. The word "you" puts accountability on me, and since it's where I have control, where I have power and things I can do right now, I feel charged up.

I think this put some rocket fuel into our conversations by igniting action. I feel charged up, so taking advantage of that energy, I head out for my rounds. I'll come back to this later in the day to take the most powerful steps I can take right now.

It's time for our next Breakthrough Forum, and I'm pleased we are now arriving on time ready to roll. I bring the team up to speed on the IdEA Model by reviewing the approach to Action I worked on with Carolyn. I explain that too often we might have the best of intentions when we name an action but end up with nothing happening. "It's like we don't anchor the solution."

LaDonna looks confused at my choice of words, and I'm a little surprised by what just came out of my mouth. I continue, "I think we have these great ideas, but we lack clarity on what we are going to do and how we are going to follow through. So the solutions are not anchored in clear action." She seems to accept that, and I even understand what I just said. So I walk through the basic elements of how we can use the Act part of our framework to create better results. I suggest the following:

✓ First, clarify action by asking for more detail. Use the Five Ws to flesh it out.

✓ Make sure we focus where we have control. Too often we don't take action because we don't feel we have control.

✓ Also, if we ask the "why" questions, we can better connect our motivations to move things forward.

I wrap up with the question Carolyn offered as a way to start actions: "What is the most powerful step to take right now?" I emphasize the key words of "most powerful" and "right now."

MAKE SURE YOU ANCHOR THE SOLUTION.

The group seems to get it. LaDonna speaks up and says, "What about follow-up? Should we have something built into our action step that deals with that?"

Now I see why she's so good at managing her projects. "Good questions. What do you all think?"

The group seems to ponder this for a moment. Bill, the controller, is first to speak up. "I don't like it when someone tells me what to do or how I'm going to do it. I also don't like when someone tells me how to follow up." I agree, it is very disempowering.

Dom agrees, a sign he and Bill are starting to work together better. "I would rather say what I'm going to do."

LaDonna comes back into the conversation and offers a simple question: "What if we ask the other person, 'How do you want to follow up with me or us?'"

Dino, the plant and maintenance manager, asks in his usual abrupt way, "What if people don't follow up? How many times do I have to chase people down for things they say they're going to do?"

The group has grown to accept his directness because he brings up those uncomfortable things we don't like to discuss. Plus, it's good to see him contributing; he had been one of those people who seemed like a reluctant passenger in our meetings.

Kim, my supervisor, says, "Sometimes we don't hear back even though someone completed what they agreed to do; they just don't close the loop. Maybe the question LaDonna offered will help that."

"And," LaDonna adds onto her statement, "maybe we can ask how they want us to respond if we don't hear back. Plus, I would suggest if someone has a habit of not following up, that is a whole conversation in and of itself."

The group seems satisfied, and I sense it's time to move on to the meeting agenda. The group has gotten very good at clearly stating the topics we're working on. They're more than problems now, but we also work on opportunities, so the meeting has a new vibe to it. The addition of the action steps only makes these conversations better. We try out some of the questions like using the Five Ws, and they help get clarity. Dino used a great question: "What hurdles are you going to run into when you are trying to do this?" The framework is working.

Chapter 7

Principles of Engagement

We've exhausted the meeting agenda and are done an hour ahead of schedule. Our agenda, and more importantly our approach to identifying issues and discussing them, has converted this meeting from a bitch session loaded with conflicts into a focused meeting on addressing real issues. We're reducing the number of recurring issues and smoothing over the underlying skirmishes, and as a result we're becoming much more efficient.

I'm about to adjourn when Jim, our head of logistics, points to the card in front of me and asks, "What's that?"

I forgot to explain the three-by-five card I have in front of me that is mounted on the alligator-clip picture holder. It helped to have the principle "Ask first, listen second, speak last" in front of me. I explain to the group how it came up in conversation and I wanted to keep it in front of me as a reminder.

I mentioned my conversation with Carl about principles of engagement as a way to give us ways to engage in better conversations. "I came up with this one to help me."

I get a puzzled look, and I'm not surprised. It sounded a little out there for a fairly technical group. I continue explaining how I want to do a better job of asking questions and listening so that principle is something I'm working on. By having it right there in front of me in our meetings and in my office, it keeps it in the forefront of my mind so I make sure I'm asking more questions and listening more often.

Jim confirms that he has seen me doing this, so it seems it's working. "I like that. Can I use that for me?"

"Sure, Jim, anyone can use this for themselves. I'm also curious what others might come up with. I'm sure there are other principles that might help us when we engage others, and each of us probably has our own areas we want to work on."

Kim says with a smile, "Hey, where can I get one of those cool alligator-clip thingies you're using for your note card?"

"I'll tell you what, if everyone likes the idea of coming up with their own principle and wants a holder like this," I say, pointing to mine, "I will buy a set for all of us." I look around the room and get several affirmations, verbal and visual. Even Joanne nods.

"Okay, next week I will bring the alligator thingies, as Kim so eloquently calls them. Let's come up with some ideas for principles you are willing to commit to for yourself when engaging others. I would emphasize that it helps to think about what you're willing to commit to, especially when we're in conflict. I've been noticing the past few days that when I'm feeling threatened, I stop asking questions and listening. And those are the moments when I probably need to ask more questions. I found it's easier to apply this when things are going smoothly."

With that, we adjourn and stick a fork in another done meeting.

At our next meeting, I'm pleased to see that people have brought three-by-five cards with them that have, what I assume to be, principles they have come up with. Some of my overachievers brought more than one. For my part, I brought the alligator-clip thingies and put one at each seat at the table.

There seems to be some energy around this, so we decide to start the meeting with the principles of engagement. I start by reiterating that the principles are for ourselves, not others, something we are willing to commit to when engaging others and being mindful of what it means when we are in conflict. I open up the floor for anyone who wants to share first.

Bill, the controller, speaks, but not with a principle. "I apologize, I don't have one. I thought about it since our last meeting, but honestly I couldn't come up with anything. I don't want you to assume I don't think it's important, it's just that my brain doesn't work that way. I'm hoping I might get some inspiration from you all as you share yours."

I appreciate his comment. "Thank you for your candor, Bill. Let's not think of this like homework. To Bill's point, I think some of us may need time to think it through. Also, I hope that as we share, we can even refine or change what we are thinking based on others people's ideas." Looking over at Sally, our head of sales operations, who has a stack of what I assume to be three cards of principles, I finish with a smile, "Plus, some of us might have more than one principle. Maybe we borrow from others."

I start by suggesting we share our principles in rapid-fire mode, along with something about what it means to that person and even why they might have selected that principle.

> **HOW CAN WE DEFINE THE PRINCIPLES WE ARE WILLING TO COMMIT TO WHEN ENGAGING EACH OTHER, ESPECIALLY WHEN WE ARE IN CONFLICT?**

I reiterate what I came up with, expanding on what it means to me and why it is important. "I'll start by sharing that I came up with my principle 'Ask first, listen second, and speak last' because I find myself jumping in with my thoughts, recommendations, and solutions before I even understand what the other person is saying." I share with humor my little anecdote that I'm going to try looping through asking and listening more than once before speaking. That gets a chuckle, so it's time for someone else.

∞ Play Good Politics ∞

Sally, our manager of sales operations, is usually pretty brave, and she jumps in next. She reveals her card like she's showing her answer on a game show and gives her best Vanna White hand wave.

The card says, "Play good politics." You can feel everyone sit forward a little in anticipation of her explanation.

She explains that she was complaining about a client who was way too political in how they worked. "My boss Peter once told me we are naturally political animals. I think he might have said he was quoting Aristotle or something. He said everyone plays politics. Honestly, I didn't want to admit that I too play politics. We all do at some level. What Peter explained to me was that there are good politics and bad politics. Good politics is for the betterment of the others, like our customers, our colleagues, our stakeholders, and our organizations. Bad politics is when what we do is for selfish reasons at the unnecessary expense of others. He said that politics is the vehicle we use to influence others, and we *have to* influence others. So I'm going to try to make sure I focus on good politics as a way to influence others for the betterment of others."

I see some nods around the room. She does a good job setting the tone. Dom, our IT manager, grabs his card as he gets ready to speak next, and I have to admit I'm worried his negativity might undo all the good Sally did starting us out.

∞ BLUF for Focus ∞

As Dom reads from his card, he says, "I really liked the acronym on our Topic-Briefing Template, BLUF or Bottom Line Up Front. I know I tend to give way too much information, and even wash over people with technical info that isn't always necessary. So just as Angela gave us the Topic-Briefing Template as a way to BLUF, I'm working on trying to create focus by framing things better anytime I communicate. Especially my emails." He chuckles. Everyone laughs along with him because it is a well-known secret that Dom has a tendency to write emails that ramble on and on with no clear action. Wow, I'm pleasantly surprised. I guess I should do a better job reserving judgment.

∞ Leverage My Gut against My Biases ∞

I wonder if Gordie, Joanne's operations manager, is reading my mind, because what he wrote relates to my response to Dom when he was about to speak. He shares a story about a boss early in his career who would ask him what his gut was telling him when they were trying to make a decision. "I'm fairly analytical, given my vocation." There's no question Gordie is a tried and true engineer, complete with a pocket protector and scientific calculator in hand wherever he goes. "So I am very uncomfortable with that statement, because it lacks facts, measurements, or data. I've been reflecting on that recently because I notice there are times in this meeting when I have this feeling in my gut that something isn't right, but I don't speak up. So the first part of my principle is 'Leverage my gut.'

"I shared this idea with my wife, and she pointed out that gut instinct is another form of data, so that helped my analytical brain. But she also challenged me to be cautious of my gut." He goes on to share that his wife works in human resources at a firm across town. I find the irony in an over-the-top engineer married to someone in HR and wonder how those dinner conversations go. "She said they have people make hiring decisions based on their gut, and they had inherent biases that would cause them to overlook qualified candidates. For example, it might have been something about their background, how they communicate, or their education, and most concerning was that they might have a bias based on factors like gender or ethnicity. I guess they spend quite a bit of time helping people understand biases for that reason. She helped me see that my gut is data, but I also need to be aware of my own biases because they are hardwired into me: I am a male, I am of a certain age," he smiles, "I am an engineer, I grew up in the Midwest, and so many more possible things about me create biases. So my final version of my principle is to leverage my gut against my biases."

∞ Socialize the Message ∞

Dino, plant and maintenance manager, jumps in. It's good to hear from him because he tends to be more reserved. He says he came up with the principle of socializing the message. "I sat down with my boss and shared with him our assignment for this meeting. He asked me, 'What is my biggest problem in my team right now?' To which I said, 'My people complain we don't communicate enough as a company.' He helped me to see that communication is a big part of my responsibility. I realized I haven't been sharing the information we've been covering in these meetings that can help them do their job, know what is coming, and feel part of the rest of the company."

He pauses for a moment and Bill, our controller, asks, "Why the word 'socialize' instead of 'communicate'?"

"Oh yeah, there was a reason for that. When I said to my boss that I thought I should write up and send my notes from this meeting, he suggested it's just as important to ask my team what they get from the information I communicate. Instead of just shoving more information at them, I think I should have some informal coffee clutches to talk about what's happening, answer questions, and most importantly hear what they might have to offer on what we're doing. Socializing the message helps to make sure we're listening." Dino clips his card to his alligator clip as a signal to whomever wants to go next.

∞ Speak My Truth ∞

LaDonna, our engineering manager, speaks next. She starts by sharing something an old boss used to say that never sat well with her. "Many of us have heard the saying 'speak truth to power.' The intent is good. We should speak up and not tamp down what we have to say just because we might be talking with someone who may have more power than we do.

"But my problem with the saying is twofold. First, when we say talk truth to power, we may assume we don't have power. I got rid of that reference because I don't want to give up the power I have. The other problem I have with that saying is that it assumes I have the truth. The minute I believe that, I've limited my ability to consider that there might be other truths. So I just simplified the saying to 'speak my truth.' That gives me permission—well, actually requires me—to share my truth. But by limiting this to my truth, I can be open to others. So I will make a more concerted effort to speak my truth in these meetings, *and* also understand."

I love LaDonna's ability to summarize something succinctly. It looks like Jim, our manager of logistics, is stepping up to the batter's box, so I glance his way.

∞ Manage the Drama ∞

Jim shares his principle, which grabs everyone's attention the minute he says it. He explains, "There is way too much drama in the logistics group. The fog of gripping and complaining is so thick you're stifled by it as you walk through the shipping area. As you can imagine, we're always under the gun. We're at the end of the chain for everything we do. Every delay and change cascades through the organization and gets dumped on our doorstep with the constant mantra 'get it out the door.' I need to find a way to manage this drama. In my twenty-five years with this company, that has never changed, and I'm not sure it ever will. Logistics is by nature an expedited business. So why all the drama?

"I've been thinking about what I can do to manage that. I come back from meetings and share with them what we discussed, and the result is this cacophony.

"Last weekend, I was rewatching *Apollo 13*, one of my favorite movies. There's a scene where they're hurtling through space after the explosion that left them in great peril. Bill Paxton's character Fred Haise and Kevin Bacon's Jack Swigert are near blows over what happened. Tom Hanks' character Jim Lovell stops them in their tracks. 'Gentleman,' he says sternly, 'what are your intentions?' They both stop and look at him. He continues, 'I'd like to go home.' In that moment, he shifted the drama from something over which they had no control to focus on something they had to do to survive. I think I need to find ways to change the focus and manage the drama."

The group is riveted, and I see Bill, who didn't have a principle, grab a three-by-five card and start writing. Jim's antidote not only captivated the group, but prompted something in Bill.

∞ Manage My Impact ∞

I've had some apprehension about Joanne participating in this exercise. Would she shoot it down? What would she come up with, if anything at all? Given her abrupt nature, I was worried about what was going to come out of her mouth. I'm reminded of Gordie's principle; I need to check my bias.

She sits forward, and the moment of truth is here. "I was sitting with my coach trying to come up with a principle." *Wait a minute,* I think, *Joanne has a professional coach?* "First, people assume things about my intent because I tend to be short and use few words. I know that might come across as abrupt, but that is just how I tend to communicate. I will never be an overly communicative person, but I'm working on rounding out some of my edges. Also, I know there are times I can be a heavy dose. I think that's part of my job, to keep people moving forward. I recognize that can keep people from speaking up. So I'm working on managing my impact in all of my conversations."

With that, Joanne is clearly done, and the group is a bit stunned in response to her self-awareness and willingness to share. Although it's her usual brusque manner, I think the group has a growing appreciation for her.

Sally says, "I think there are times we make assumptions about people's intent when we don't really know. I think we should be cautious about assuming someone's intent. I've seen too many problems arise from those faulty assumptions."

∞ Be a Control Freak ∞

Bill looks ready to share what he came up with, and I'm curious what inspired him from what Jim was saying. He says, "I need to be a control freak," and I can see the group is as concerned as I am that Bill missed the point. Relief comes as he explains.

"When Jim was talking, I realized there are so many times we focus on those things we don't have control over. It's like dogs barking at the moon; the moon never changes or moves when they're howling. There are times I can do the same thing. Last week I was flying back from a conference, and my flight was cancelled. Me and a couple of hundred other people were sitting in the terminal barking at the moon. I realized, after Jim was talking, we were focusing on what we don't have control over. So let me ask you, did I have any control in that situation?"

Everyone shakes their head no.

"Let me bend our minds a little. I think I did have control. So let's explore where I might have had control." The conversation gains some momentum as first one person, then another, starts offering ways he had control, like he could have looked for alternate flights, he could have rented a car, he could have looked for flights to a nearby airport and driven home from there, and so on. The group even offered ways he had control when planning the trip. Gordie noted that he was flying through Chicago in the winter, and he avoids that connection that time of year for that reason. Jim, given his logistics background, points out that delays and cancellations cascade through the day, so by taking the last flight, he increased his risk of a cancellation.

Sally puts the icing on the conversation by pointing out, "Even if you're stuck, you have control over how you choose to react, even over other people you choose to interact with. When I get delayed, I head to the bar. Everyone at the terminal complains, but the people in the bar are more fun. I might as well have fun." With that, everyone laughs.

Bill finishes by saying, "Jim helped me think about how I can keep my focus on where I have control. So although some of you thought I was going to be amping up my control freakishness, my principle is not what you think it means." Everyone has a good belly laugh.

∞ Increase Your CQ ∞

Kim is our last person to contribute. "I stole my principles shamelessly from Angela." She nods to me. "And in some ways, it's similar to her principle, 'Ask first, listen second, speak last.'"

Kim goes to the whiteboard and writes the CQ equation for everyone to see.

$$Curiosity\ Quotient = \left(\dfrac{Questions\ Asked}{Statements\ Made} \right) Mutual\ Understanding$$

"Even though it's similar to Angela's principle, I like how it's an equation reminding me to balance the questions I ask with the statements I make." She explains that the idea of an equation helps her to think about the uniqueness of each situation and to be mindful of the ratio of questions she is asking to statements she is making.

"There are times when I need to make statements, like providing direction and setting expectations. However, I need to interweave them with questions. Honestly, there are more situations where I lead with statements when I would be better served by asking a lot more questions. So that's why I wrote this as increasing my CQ. Like an IQ to represent intelligence, or EQ, the term people use to represent emotional intelligence, I think I can have a much better CQ."

"Thank you, Kim," I say. "Wow, that is quite a list of principles. What do you all think?" There is some good, affirming conversation. So for something I worried would end up like a face-plant, it generated some good ideas.

There is some discussion about using other people's principles, which seems like a good idea. Joanne shares that her coach recommended that, although she might be working on more than one thing for her professional development, she might keep the focus on one or a few things. Given that, she suggests we have these printed in a nice, laminated card deck so we can keep them handy. I think to myself, *Did Joanne just offer something like this for the whole group? That's out of character.* The group seems to like the idea.

Sally, who came with more than one card, says, "I actually came up with three cards, but only shared one. If we have it printed as a deck, would it be worth adding these in?"

Joanne asks, "What have you got?" Sally takes it as a genuine interest, when normally that type of curt question would be seen as a challenge.

∞ Be Direct with Respect ∞

She says the first one, revealing a card with the phrase "Be direct with respect," came to her because of an interaction with a member of her team last week. "This guy has a direct style that can be off putting. When you challenge him, he says he is just being direct, which implies it's okay. I realized after the meeting that being direct is okay, but there has to be level respect for the other person. That means respecting who they are, their style, their needs, and their perspectives."

∞ Kick But ∞

"The second one came to me during one of my staff meetings. We have this one person who tends to 'yeah, but' me. Anytime I, or someone else, say something, his response starts with 'yeah, but' or something of that derivation. I never understood why it makes my blood boil until I realized when he does his 'yeah, but,' my interpretation is that his 'but' —" she spells out B-U-T—"comes across to me as very devaluing.

"In last week's meeting, I was able to bring it up in a way that didn't call out this person. I found out that other people had the same reaction, and that all of us have a tendency to overuse the word 'but.' One of my teammates worked in theater in college and offered an exercise he learned in an improv class. They use 'and' to help people build and create ideas and storylines. He shared that when we use 'but,' we are actually deconstructing and tearing down. He said you can replace the word 'but' with the word 'and' in any sentence and still have the same meaning.

"He suggested that as a team, we start replacing the word 'but' with 'and.' We tried it in the meeting and found out how insidious that word is, how much it creeps into our language. When we caught ourselves using the word 'and,' the energy, focus, and creativity in the room changed. So that's why I wrote the 'Kick But' principle."

BUT DECONSTRUCTS, AND BUILDS UP.

Joanne, since she invited Sally to share the two principles, says, "I like 'em, I say add 'em." Even though she didn't ask the group, I look around and see heads nodding.

Sally offers to have the entire set of principles formatted and printed on nice stock, like playing cards. "Everyone will get a full set." She asks and gets confirmation that the group would like to have the author's name on each principle. She says, "I will have the last two labelled as wild cards."

Joanne offers one more thought for the group, which only continues the streak of pleasant surprises. "One thing you might think about as you work on improving around the principle you created is picking something you will do differently. My coach says to identify one strategy you might try. Don't try to do too much." With that, she looks to me and the message is it's time to move on.

That took a little longer than expected, but it seems that was a significant step in laying some guardrails for the group. I reflect on my conversation with Carl a few weeks ago, when we talked about setting boundaries for how we engage in conflict. I look down at the list of principles I captured from everyone, and I'm very impressed.

Everyone now has clipped their card on the alligator thingy I brought them. It's time to turn our attention to the business at hand.

Chapter 8

What about Feedback?

It's been a couple of months since we defined conflict, created the IdEA framework, came up with our principles of engagement, and defined the Topic-Briefing Template. Peter is paying me a visit to bring my daily dose of caffeine in what has become an informal ritual. Since he has never asked for that big favor, I'm no longer guarded when we talk. Anyway, at this point he's been such a great supporter and offered so many great ideas, he could ask for anything and I would happily oblige.

We're catching up, casually reflecting on the progress we have made as a team. "You've done a good job, Angela, getting the group talking about the important things we need to talk about as a team."

As he elaborates, I smile a little with that self-satisfaction we so rarely allow ourselves. I'm also aware that it hasn't been without its challenges. There have been plenty of places where we hit walls as a team. For example, I still get the feeling that people hesitate to raise challenges out of fear. The fears can be many: for example, getting called out, calling out someone else, being wrong, being the lightning rod for a conversation, and the ultimate fear of being fired.

It is also clear that asking good questions takes time and practice. There are still times when someone thinks they're asking a question, but it's really a direction. That proverbial wolf in sheep's clothing can sound like this: "Have you thought about telling engineering to reprioritize?" There are also times I hear judgment loaded into questions like, "How can we get the customers to stop trying to cheap out on us?"

Peter builds on what I'm saying: "It reminds me of a quote I heard once about questions. 'The more open ended the question, the more potential.' The point is that when we have close-ended questions like, 'Have you thought of . . .,' 'Did you ask so-and-so . . .,' and 'What about this idea . . .,' we are limiting the potential that can come from conversation. So alternative questions that are more open ended can be, 'What else are you thinking of? Who else can give you insight to this?' and 'What other ideas have you considered?'"

Because I like equations, I write it as "More open ended = More potential." Peter is reading what I'm writing in my journal upside down across the table. "Another equation." He smiles. "You are becoming an engineer, aren't you? Engineering conversations, equations for curiosity quotients, and now an algebraic equation for questions." I smile and make a note to myself: "Add this to principles of engagement?" I will have to bring that up at our next meeting.

MORE OPEN ENDED = MORE POTENTIAL.

I continue my summary for Peter. "We've made great progress getting some tough discussions on the table. For example, we've tackled the special request backlog crisis and even put in place a process to handle special requests going forward. Bill, our controller, and Dom, our head of IT, seem to be getting along better. I even sense that the team appreciates Dom more now that they understand he's pointing out risks. And Dom, for his part, has moved past just pointing out risks to offering constructive ideas."

I let him know that Joanne still attends the meetings, but with less frequency. She still has her hawkish eyes always on alert for something. It's a bit unsettling, but I've gotten used to it. Plus, I know she's trying to "manage her impact," as she pointed out by the principle she created. I've learned that part of it is just her posture. I can see her trying to do better. She can actually be pretty engaging, and she seems to have eased up on me a bit. I don't get those sharp elbows as much, and when I do, I'm able to write it off as her style. I listen to what she is saying and worrying less about how she is saying it. She seems to be letting go and not trying to drive everything. Even the rest of the group seems to work well with her in the room.

I say to Peter, "I'm pleased with the number of topics the team has tackled together. They've been doing a much better job teeing up topics using the Topic-Briefing Template you helped me create. Of course, it has been great to see people bring the template in with notes ready to engage in healthy discussion. I am also pleased because there are times something comes up and people grab a copy of the blank template I have at the ready. Sometimes they jot notes to prepare to bring up a topic, other times they use it as an outline when they talk extemporaneously. All in all, we've gotten much better about naming the gap." I look to the poster in my office that has the conflict definition.

"And I've seen the group doing yeoman's work making sure they understand all the different perspectives," Peter adds as he looks at the definition. "I remember the last time I was in a meeting, I watched the group asking questions around the five areas of Explore. It wasn't linear, it just flowed. Someone would ask a data question, and that would prompt someone else to ask a risk question that would lead people to explore motivation. It seems like this is a mindset, not a process they have to follow.

"What I really appreciate is that the focus of the team on actions and performance has improved significantly. Which is why I brought you this dinner certificate as a thank-you. We've been battling the special request problem for ages. You and the team have made my life imminently easier, and more importantly, it has helped with revenues, costs, and better profits."

I'm shocked, and I'm sure he sees it in my face. This is way more than the coffees he's been bringing me the past months. I start to object. "This wasn't just me, it was really a team effort."

"I thought about that, and that is why there's enough on that certificate to take the entire team to the Brass Rail and let them bring significant others. You should all have a chance to celebrate."

I'm overwhelmed. "Thank you, that is very kind and generous of you."

"This isn't just from me. The team's progress has been a topic of discussion at the executive committee meetings. Everyone is aware of the team's work, as I have been sharing with them the progress and what you've put in place. Your definition of conflict is actually in the middle of the executive conference room table in a small table tent. We have also reviewed your IdEA framework, and we're using it when we talk about important topics. We have even been using the Topic-Briefing Template.

"I would say it's been helpful for us, but the executive committee and Gayle, our illustrious president, want you to come to our next meeting and review everything you've done and share your learning. We want to continue to improve how we're using these ideas and tools."

Holy crap! screams out in my head. Well, I guess the saying is true, there is no such thing as a free lunch, or in this case a free dinner. My stomach has dropped to my toes, and I think Peter sees my hand visibly shaking.

"Look, don't panic. I'll help you get ready." He gets up to head out of my office. "I'll get back to you to set up a time to prep."

With that, he has left me with a pit the size of a boulder sitting square in my belly. I won't be able to eat anything until this thing is over.

Well, I guess that can be my forced diet plan.

It's been a few weeks since Carl and I have spoken. I give him an update and fill him in on Peter's request to brief the executive team on what we've been doing. I share with him how the executive meeting went. Overall, I was honored they asked, and it wasn't just a fluffy accolade that brought me to the meeting. They are generally interested in what we've been doing.

I had lots of question about what we've done and how we did it, as well as challenges we faced and continue to face. Gayle shared that the executive team has been watching this group. Not only to see how we're progressing, but also trying out the tools and concepts. I noticed the definition of conflict in the middle of the table, and several of the executive team had topics outlined for their meeting using the Topic-Briefing Template.

"I also got an assignment from the meeting."

"What's that?" he asks.

"I have to come back with a recommendation on how we can leverage these tools and concepts throughout the organization. Gayle reinforced that it's important we all have common language and common tools. Since we've proven what we created, she wants to influence that across the organization. She did ask to avoid the tendency to build more procedures and bureaucracy. I feel good about this and think it's very doable."

"And . . . ?" he asks, sensing there's more.

"And she wants me to tackle another challenge. She says that although we have a performance review process, she's concerned that we're not good at giving and receiving timely feedback as an organization. She wonders if what we did in the Breakthrough Forum can provide a foundation for building better, more robust feedback loops in the moment.

"She used the analogy of the manufacturing process in our plant to explain that for a plant to run well, it needs rapid feedback to make adjustments. Gayle said good performance needs the same thing. We can't wait for annual reviews, or even the quarterly touchpoints we're supposed to be doing. I didn't think this was the place to tell her the quarterly touchpoints oftentimes get sacrificed at the altar of the urgent. Gayle pointed out, using the definition of conflict, feedback is an area that might also be creating conflict. I think she's on to something but I'm not sure what."

> **FAILURE IN FEEDBACK CREATES MORE CONFLICT. RAPID AND ROBUST FEEDBACK LOOPS CAN REDUCE CONFLICT.**

He says, "I like the language of feedback loops. Also, the manufacturing-process analogy is in parallel with how you came up with your IdEA Model for conversations."

"Feedback loops are pretty straightforward. You do something, you measure it against some set of expectations, provide feedback when it doesn't match, readjust, and do it again." I'm doodling a loop on my pad as I talk. His use of the word "expectation" ties back to our definition: "A gap between what we expect and what we experience . . ."

"That seems pretty straightforward," he says. "So how does that translate to performance?"

"I think that means when something is out of whack with our expectations, we need to get that feedback quickly. But something is different than our manufacturing process."

"What's that?"

"We don't have machines breaking down in tears, getting defensive, or going into therapy because we gave it feedback."

He laughs a hearty laugh.

"Plus, measuring a product's quality is much easier than measuring the effectiveness of an interaction at work. The standards are different from person to person," I continue.

He lets the silence sit there as I think this through, which is what I need to do. "We probably need to be more deliberate in how we give feedback. I think that's the key. Too many times, people bring in feedback like a ninja star, flinging it as we sail by someone and not worrying about sticking them with the blades.

"Last week in our meeting, I heard someone from manufacturing tell Dom he really screwed something up and needed to fix it. There were a number of problems with that, like where he delivered the feedback, but also what he said. If he had said that to someone serving him food, I'd be concerned he'd get his meal with a sneezer."

He laughs again and says, "Makes sense. I have to run, but I would love to hear what you do with this."

We hang up, and I stare at the poster of the IdEA conversational framework: Identify, Explore, Act. How does feedback fit into that process?

— ∞ —

As I stare at the IdEA framework, my eye keeps going to the word "Identify." It seems we need to do a better job of identifying the feedback versus the haphazard way we do it today. I go to the whiteboard and write "feedback" at the top. Underneath, I write, "Name it." That's it, we need to name it better. But it seems there should be more. First, we can't just name it like the person did to Dom. For example, "You screwed that up." That isn't naming it, that's an overt attack.

I drum my fingers on the guest table in my office with my chin in hand, staring at the whiteboard. I'm so absorbed I don't hear the wheels of Carolyn's cart or her footsteps as she comes by my office.

Observing my position and focus, she says in her jovial way, "If you're trying to move your whiteboard telepathically, I would suggest it's futile because it's screwed to the wall."

"Got a minute?"

"Sure," she says.

I give her the basic overview of the challenge to provide better feedback, the idea of a feedback loop, and using the IdEA Model to name it better. She nods along. "I know we need to name it better, but I'm not sure what's in the name." I share with her the situation with Dom. I understood the frustration, but the way he delivered the feedback wasn't going to help him, me, or the project.

"Maybe step back for a minute and ask a few questions first before you give feedback. What do you need to know?" She points to the poster with the definition of conflict on my wall.

CONFLICT: A GAP BETWEEN WHAT WE <u>EXPECT</u> AND WHAT WE <u>EXPERIENCE</u> THAT LEADS TO DEEPER <u>UNDERSTANDING</u> AND BETTER <u>RESULTS</u>.

"I guess I need to see the gap" —I pause— "between what we expected and what we experienced?"

"So the first question is what you expected and what you experienced. Think about listing out what you observed."

I walk through what happened with this project, and it becomes clearer. "I expected him to loop back with the manufacturing people before he implemented the new software to make sure it was doing what it was supposed to do without having a negative impact on them. Instead, he just launched the new code, and although it did exactly what we asked, it made manufacturing's job harder because they had to have someone manually enter commands while a job was running."

"So . . ." She invites me to continue.

"We got the usual response, 'I did exactly what the spec said,' which makes my head spontaneously combust, and then manufacturing starts chucking harpoons.

"This degraded into a game of point bludgeoning, where one side bludgeons the other, going back and forth until someone is knocked down and bloody. After a few rounds, Dom threw his hands up, saying, 'Look, I do exactly what you tell me.' Now we have what I call arms and legs compliance—he will do what he's told, but nothing more, nothing less. I know this guy is smart; I don't know why he doesn't anticipate some of these things."

Carolyn prompts me. "So if you were to name this issue, what would you call it?"

"Originally, I would have said the issue was this particular project, but now I think it's more about how we manage these projects between customer service, IT, and any other departments. And ultimately, how we define and manage these specifications together."

"So I think you have two of the key pieces: you named it and have an example." She has written on the whiteboard underneath where I had written "Name it," so it now says.

NAME IT
EXAMPLE(S)

"So the one piece we're missing is the 'why.' The reason people might not make a change when we're giving feedback is because there is no 'why' for them. Too many times, we talk about the 'why' for the project, the company, the customer, or any other host of reasons. They might not care about those reasons, but we all care about what is important to us. What we need to do is name why it's important to them. So why would this be important to Dom?" With that, she goes to the board and writes, "Why," underneath "Name it" and "Example(s)" so it now says:

NAME IT
EXAMPLE(S)
WHY

"The obvious answers are things like his job and his performance review. But I think it needs to be something else. I noticed his frustration in the meeting, so the 'why' for him might be related to his frustration or how he feels about the projects he's working on. There's definitely more to what's going on, and I'm not sure why he's not happy with the projects."

"So what would you name as a 'why' for him?"

"Because it might be impacting his satisfaction with the projects he's working on and how he feels about his job." As I say that, I realize I never thought about what's in it for them.

"So put it all together."

I'm surprised at how easily it flows out of my mouth and how succinct it is. "I wanted to talk about how we work together managing project specifications. I noticed in our last meeting you were frustrated when we talked about the code problem in manufacturing. I think this might be impacting how we're working together, how you feel about your work, and the projects you work on."

I notice the three words Carolyn has written on the whiteboard spell NEW: Name it, Example(s), and Why. That should make it easy to remember how to give feedback.

Okay, I'm ready to go talk with Dom. But I notice that Carolyn sees this in my face, and something says there's more to think about. "So what am I missing?"

She points to my note card, where it says, "Ask first, listen second, speak last." "I wonder where that might come into play when you are giving feedback?"

With that, she gathers herself to head out. "Gotta run, but I look forward to hearing how you might incorporate your principle into feedback."

After I've written my NEW statement neatly in my journal, I look at my note card and wonder how to incorporate "asking" and "listening before speaking." My first reaction is to rush down the hall and deliver my brilliant little statement to Dom. But I know there's something missing.

I draw my feedback loop again and realize that, first, I might want to ask the other person how things are going. Too often I think it's necessary to give people feedback, but like the situation with Dom, I'm sure they have a better sense of how things are going without me telling them. I'm sure if the moment presented itself and I were genuinely interested, they would tell me, versus me having to tell them. I just need to extend the invitation in a gracious way.

I remember a former boss telling me that too many times we think we need to inflict our feedback on others. There are some flawed assumptions in giving feedback, like whether the other person is ready to hear it, we know what's going on, we know what's best, and a whole host more. I remember a former boss telling me our goal is not to run around and give feedback, it's to help others accurately self-assess so they don't need our feedback. I jot that thought in my journal: "Creating feedback loops can help others accurately self-assess."

He also said, "Stop asking people how you can help them." That idea shocked me because we had been trained as leaders to ask our people how we can help them. What he said was that when you ask how you can help someone, you end up collecting action items, so you're only making your job more difficult. It's also a

CONFLICT IS NOT SOMETHING WE INFLICT ON OTHERS.

bit egotistical to assume you can actually help them. But more importantly, you're disempowering other people because the underlying assumption is that they need your help. We want people to feel they can work independently without us. So he suggested asking instead, "What help do you need?"

At that exact moment, Dom walks into my office. He must have seen me burning the midnight oil. Since he has his backpack over his shoulder, I assume he wanted to stop and say goodnight on his way out. I invite him to sit for a minute if he has time; he obliges willingly. I think he's interested in connecting outside of the usual daily flurry of activity. I toss him a water bottle as I wheel over to my guest table.

I'm thinking about my NEW statement and giving him the feedback I prepared, but I resist the temptation, and boy does it takes a lot of energy to resist. I figure I should start with a question that might get him talking.

"Hey, I was curious, what was your take on the meeting the other day about the new manufacturing code?"

He slumps in his chair, and I wonder if the timing was right. But he does respond. "These freaking projects are driving me nuts." So I know he sees it. I just need to listen. As we talk about what happened, I learn quite a bit more about the source of his frustration. First, when he asks for clarification on specifications, he gets vague answers. That leaves him guessing what the program should do. Then when it's done, everyone becomes a critic.

"Why didn't you test it out with the floor?" I wonder out loud, because that's the major problem.

"I did, or I should say, I tried."

"What do you mean?"

"I tried to schedule something with the manufacturing manager who requested the update, and he kept blowing me off. He sent me to one of his minions, who gave me a blanket 'Looks good to me.' So I let it rip. If I'm to be honest with you, I knew there were risks to this, but I've gotten so frustrated I've given up. Then he comes into our last meeting telling me how I screwed it up."

> **THERE IS ALWAYS MORE TO THE STORY.**

"That sounds like it must be very frustrating to you," I say, consoling him a bit. It seems to open him up a bit more as he goes on to explain how often he has these types of situations.

"So I've gotten to the point where I make sure I do what's requested, to cover my ass and let the chips fall where they may. Honestly, I hate that I'm reduced to doing that. And when something goes wrong, whether it's my fault or not, it makes me hate my job." He's genuinely contrite, and I'm honored he would be this open with me.

I can see why he drops into that passive-aggressive mode so easily. I would too if I were getting beaten into hopelessness. It's also a reminder of an axiom my father used to say: "There is always more to the story." He would use hockey as a way to illustrate. "You see, the guy who gets the penalty is not the one who throws the punch; it's the one who throws the punch back."

We talk a bit longer, and it seems our conversation has provided a cathartic effect on Dom. Even though we haven't come to some mystical solution, I can feel his energy elevate. Like my former boss told me, it's presumptuous to assume I know what he should do. Of course I have some ideas, but now isn't the time or the place for me to try to be the all-knowing orb.

I look at the IdEA Model and realize we've done a good job identifying and we spent a good amount of time exploring. I wonder if Carolyn will give me my gold star for asking and listening before speaking.

Sensing that Dom has exhausted this conversation and is ready to call it a day, I wonder how to incorporate action. Recognizing that it's not my action to name or take, I ask him. "So, where do you want to go with this?"

Continuing with his vulnerability and honesty, he says, "I know the way I've been handling these situations isn't working. I guess I need to find a new way to work on these projects when the specs aren't clear and I don't get the support from the customer or end user. I need to go think about it a bit."

"I know this is important to you, and I'm interested in knowing how it comes together for you. Would you let me know how it's coming along?"

"Sure!" I think he's happy someone is interested and listening.

Not wanting to lose momentum and be left wondering if anything happened, I press our action one step further. "How would you like to follow up and when?"

"Would you mind if I scheduled a meeting for us next week? I appreciate you listening, and I'll probably be ready to puzzle through some ideas by then."

"Sounds like a plan," I say as he heads out the door with a little more energy than when he entered.

Carolyn passes by again a few minutes after Dom has left and I hail her down. "Hey, I have to let you know about the conversation I just had Dom." I fill her in and even brag a little about asking and listening. "But I'm curious, we just outlined this feedback for Dom using the NEW framework, and I never had to use it. Did I waste my time?"

She thinks at the same time as me, and although she might have an answer, she doesn't provide it, letting me think about it. "I guess it's better if the other person says it, versus me saying it. That way they own it. But this way, I'm prepared if they don't bring it up and

I need to provide that feedback. Also, I noticed Dom named what's motivating—or more realistically, demotivating—him, which was job satisfaction. So he identified his 'why' and what would motivate him."

IF THE OTHER PERSON IDENTIFIES IT, THEY OWN IT.

She says, "I think it makes sense that you might prepare the feedback and not use it. Without knowing, it sounds like Dom named it, gave examples, and even gave the 'why.' Being prepared might help you or how you can help the other person frame it. Also, it sounds like you would be prepared to provide the feedback if the other person doesn't bring it up."

As she talks, I draw another loop in my feedback loop that shows providing feedback if the other person doesn't name it.

"Plus," Carolyn adds, "Just by taking the time to prepare the feedback, you might find you're more comfortable providing direct and specific feedback in other situations. Practice makes perfect," she says with a smile. "But I sense there's something else you're thinking about."

"I'm thinking about Dom, who, because of how IT is treated, has become everyone's whipping boy. Everyone points out what our software doesn't do, or when it's wrong. But no one ever gives IT credit for when it goes right. Actually, I think that's probably true for many of us."

"We assume feedback is only critical, and we don't recognize how important positive feedback is for others," Carolyn confirms. "Creating a culture of feedback requires both positive and constructive feedback."

I take note of her word choice: "culture of feedback." It's something I need to think about more, so I jot it in my journal to put a pin in it later.

I continue with our thread. "But when we give positive feedback, it tends to be so general it's fluffy. We tend to criticize specifically, but praise generally. People think saying, 'Nice job,' is enough. Although it is nice to hear that, it doesn't do enough."

"Why would we deliver positive feedback differently than we would deliver constructive feedback?" she asks, glancing up to the whiteboard where we had outlined our feedback method NEW.

CREATE A CULTURE OF FEEDBACK.

"Hmm, great point. I guess it needs the same thing: to be named clearly, to show examples so they know what it was you noticed, and even why it's important to them." I continue to ponder. "What just occurred to me is that by being specific, not only do we increase the impact of positive feedback, we help people see what they did well so they're more likely to do it again."

"Great point," she says, and with that she's bounding out of my office. Her voice trails after her. "I should let you get on with your work so you can get out of here. Love your thinking here, I can't wait to hear what you do with it."

Left alone with my thoughts, I realize I need to provide some positive feedback for Dom. He has really worked hard to be a more positive contributor in our meetings. I've also seen him using his BLUF principle to succinctly name topics. Although he still sends epistles in email, he always starts with a good BLUF summary up front that clearly names the topic of the email, a couple of key points, and what he wants from the email. The group has also responded positively to his efforts.

I pull out my journal and try writing out what I might say to him using the NEW framework:

> *Dom, I wanted to commend your efforts applying your BLUF principle. I am not the only one who has benefited from your succinct summary of topics in our meetings. I've also noticed your emails are reflecting the same cogent summaries. This is really powerful because people understand what you are facing and are more able to respond to your needs.*

I look at what I just scrawled with a sense of self-satisfaction. Hey, that wasn't so hard. I should do this more often. I close my journal for the day, resolved to make sure I see Dom tomorrow and rain some sunshine on his day.

PROVIDING POS-ITIVE FEEDBACK REQUIRES THE SAME DISCIPLINE AND LEVEL OF DETAIL.

On, Sunday morning, the mid-winter sun shines through my dining room window, warming me along with the steam rising off my coffee. My phone rings and Carl greets me with one of his many nicknames: "Dudette." To which I reply, "Sup," the two of us trying to sound hip and neither pulling it off. We both chuckle at ourselves.

"I wanted to follow up on our conversation about feedback loops. I'm sorry I had to cut it short the other day. How's it coming?"

I share with him the NEW framework and both the constructive and positive examples I created for Dom. I had already stopped by to see Dom and provided the positive feedback as a NEW statement.

"I'm not sure who benefited more, him or me. It was a jolt to Dom, but an energizing jolt. You would think he'd just won the lottery. I realized he, like many of us, gets positive feedback so infrequently, it can feel like you hit the lottery. But I also think that being specific helped amp up the feedback. For my part, I got my own jolt because it was nice to see someone about something other than a complaint and also know I had a positive impact on them. I realize I need to find more opportunities to do that using the framework."

I also share with him my reflections from my previous boss about inflicting feedback and our need to help others accurately: "self-assess."

Carl is genuinely complimentary of what we have so far. He builds on my experience by sharing a personal anecdote.

"I was thinking about your task of building feedback loops when I was playing golf with my son. I realize that too often I'm ready to jump in with advice on where to improve. Also, I don't compliment him enough. But I also realized I don't ask him how he's doing from his perspective. So yesterday when we were playing golf, I tried something different." Now he's rubbing in my choice to move back where the snow flies while he enjoys a warm day out west. "Instead of telling him how I think he's doing, maybe I should ask him. I started by asking him how he thought he was doing to see how he could 'self-assess,' as you put it. The problem I ran into was that he jumped in to tell me everything that went wrong."

As he shares his story, I realize how often that happens: we ask someone how it's going and we end up hearing or talking about our problems.

"So I changed the question and started by asking what he did well. It wasn't natural for him, but he did say he thought he was putting well. I didn't stop there, I asked him how he was able to putt better and what he had been doing. He shared with me that he's spending more time on the putting green and trying out some new putting drills he found online. He said this helped him more than trying to hit the big clubs on the driving range. He said there are more putts per round than drives. Not only do I think that helped reinforce what he was doing, but I learned something. I went home and looked up the putting drills so I could learn from his experience. I also realized how often I get it wrong when talking with my people at work. I'm missing both opportunities to help people reinforce what they're doing well, and opportunities to learn from them."

As he shares his story, I add notes to the feedback loop I've been drawing in my notebook. It's really starting to take form. I now have two side-by-side loops, one for positive feedback, the other for constructive feedback. Also, just like my principle, "Ask first," I realize if we want to build robust feedback loops, it isn't about us inflicting our feedback on others, but helping people self-assess. In the center, I've drawn a box to explore. To make sure we explore, just like our IdEA Model, we need to ask more questions.

"But what if we have constructive feedback, like your son's golf game? Let's say you notice something he's either doing well or needs to improve that he didn't mention." I ask the question as much for Carl as for myself. Answering my own question and finishing the thought in my head, I say, "I think it's important to listen first."

> PEOPLE ARE MORE RECEPTIVE TO YOUR FEEDBACK IF YOU LISTEN FIRST.

"And," Carl adds, "I think people are more likely to be receptive to your feedback if you've listened first. Then, if you need to offer your feedback, I think you can interject using your NEW statement."

I've added to my loop, so now it seems to represent a more robust feedback loop.

The Self-Assessment Feedback Loop

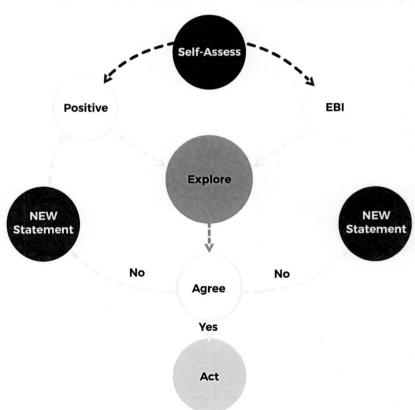

"Can I steal shamelessly from you?" he asks. "I want to try this out with my team. As a matter of fact, I have a meeting tomorrow with one of my project managers to talk about the project he's working on. I think I can use this with him."

"Sure. I'll take a picture of the loop I've drawn and send it to you. The price of using this for yourself is that you have to update me on how it goes and share anything you learn."

"That's a cheap cost. Consider it done. I'll buzz you later this week."

We wrap up our call, and I take an action to use this feedback loop with Kim in our next one-on-one when we talk about her projects. It will help me to practice my principle of asking first if I start by asking her perspective first and really exploring what she has to say. That will change our conversations from ones of review and checking homework to ones of building both of our understanding.

Chapter 9

Confrontation

Peter and I are in my office doing our informal coffee clutch and catch-up. It's been several months and he has never asked for that "big favor" I kept expecting. He's been a true confidant, mentor, and supporter. I'm getting ready for an update with the executive team on the challenge Gayle gave me on building feedback loops as a way to reduce or mitigate conflict.

I walk him through the NEW framework we created to deliver feedback. He likes the simplicity, and it makes it easy to remember. He also likes that it includes providing detailed positive feedback. He agrees we don't do a good job of "anchoring the behavior" when people do things well.

"The idea of helping people self-assess is a unique angle. I can see that we think of feedback as something we give to others versus helping them do it themselves," he says, confirming the approach. "So what do you do when you have to confront something difficult? Would you follow the same loop?"

"I've been thinking about that, but I'm not quite sure yet. I want to keep the same simplicity we have with the IdEA framework, the Topic-Briefing Template, and the NEW framework. I'm afraid if we create something different for confrontation, it will confuse the issue. Besides, confrontation is just feedback on steroids."

I open my journal to something I've been doodling around levels of feedback. "I think feedback falls on a spectrum. On one end, we have observational feedback. That can be pretty easy because the stakes are probably lower, the impact is lower, and emotions are lower. We can usually deal with those situations by using our feedback loops. But as stakes, impact, and emotions increase, I think it requires a more direct approach. For example, as we move up the spectrum to higher intensity, if we ask someone how things are going when we really intend to give them some directed feedback, it can come across as disingenuous, or worse, seem like a setup."

FEEDBACK FALLS ON A SPECTRUM FROM OBSERVATIONAL FEEDBACK TO CONFRONTATION.

Peter agrees. "I think your same basic NEW structure can work. You still need to name it succinctly and without the load. My guess is you might have more examples, maybe even a whole list of examples you've been accumulating. And you still need to address why it's important to them to make a change. So I think you can build on that. I would also assume you can ask yourself the same questions you outlined for feedback, like what have you seen, experienced, and observed. So what do you think is different?"

"Clearly I need to take more time to prepare, because my emotions are going to be pretty high." I haven't shared with him a conflict I ran into with Joanne in a meeting recently. I'm fairly jacked up about it, and I haven't felt like I'm in a place to broach the subject with her. Especially since she's my senior. At the same time, what she did undermined me in front of the group. "I also think I'm less likely to want to hear the other person's perspective since my emotions are hijacking me." I reflect on Joanne again, thinking, *I don't care what reason she had for doing what she did, what she did is unacceptable.*

I make a few notes in my journal as Peter talks, even though I want to put on my armor of righteousness and go after Joanne.

Confrontation:

✓ Ask yourself the same questions as feedback. What did you see, hear, or experience, and why it is important to them?

✓ Requires more time to prepare and deescalate my emotions.

✓ Be open to hearing the other person's perspective.

"One of the questions you might want to consider is, 'Why are your emotions hijacking you?'" he suggests.

Ouch, I think. *I wasn't ready to see that through the smoke of my righteousness.*

He continues, "Oftentimes we get hijacked not because of what happened, but because of some underlying meaning to you or what you've assumed about the other person."

I think he might see my hesitation because of how I'm feeling about the situation with Joanne.

"Look," he continues, "I admit I didn't handle it well the other day when one of my salespeople showed up for my meeting late, yet again. To me, it wasn't about him being late. That can happen to anyone. It was that his continual lateness triggered me in another way. I had this whole list of things running through my head, like he's being disrespectful, he thinks he's more important than everyone else, and he isn't committed to our weekly report. So in these situations, I try to remember what a boss used to ask me: 'What's this about for you?' In this case, it wasn't about the lateness, but the intent I ascribed to his lateness."

"What if he really is disrespectful?" I ask.

"The thing is, I don't know what his intention is or what's behind it. So what I did in this case, because I let myself get hijacked, is make a snide remark. I actually said, 'So, did we oversleep today?' Now I've made myself look bad and put everyone else on the defensive.

"These triggers are so naturally ingrained in us that oftentimes we react without understanding what's actually triggering us. I've found over time as I take time to reflect on these triggers, I'm more likely to keep them from hijacking me. As demonstrated by my response to my salesperson, I obviously need to continue working on this."

So I add it to my confrontation notes.

✓ What's this about for me, what's hijacking me, what's triggering me?

"So it seems to me I need to make sure that as we move up the intensity scale, I need to take time to self-reflect a bit," I agree with him.

"Let me lay another one on you that you might want to consider. And this one is going to be tougher. The same boss who would ask what it was about for me would also ask, 'So where is your hand-print on the crime scene?'"

Well, that cut me to my core, and Peter can see me tighten up a bit at even considering what I might have contributed.

"I know that isn't something we're used to considering. My father used to say, 'It takes two to tango.' Which was his way of saying both parties have some responsibility. In the case of my sales rep, there are probably multiple ways I contributed to this situation. The most obvious is that I hadn't addressed it sooner. But after I reflected on it even more, I realized I hadn't really set a clear expectation, and I hadn't reinforced it because it seems like someone is late each week. He could have seen it as acceptable. Plus, I have to admit there are times I am late and leave the team waiting for me."

I decide to come clean with him and tell him what happened with Joanne, because everything he's saying, although uncomfortable, is also true. I need to think this through, and I feel I can trust him to keep it confidential. I explain that in our last meeting, Joanne had an outburst that undermined me as the meeting leader and unraveled some of the progress we've made as a team. We were at the end of our agenda covering any other topics people needed to discuss that weren't covered in the regular agenda. I admitted this segment had turned into a bit of an unfocused bitch session. "Joanne burst out in front of everyone, 'Can we get on with this?' And on top of her outburst, she continued to ladle on her scorn. 'Honestly, this is like grammar school, I have better things to do with my time.'

"Everyone shut down, the meeting ended, and people skulked out of the meeting room. This will sit in the middle of our meeting like a huge pink elephant, squashing conversations unless we do something. If I'm honest with you, I did sense something bothering her during this segment. She tends to scowl a bit more, crosses her arms, she even rolls her eyes at times. I see it, and I know others can see it too. So I guess I'm not that surprised at her outburst."

Peter adds, "I know there are times we act surprised, but really, we aren't surprised at all."

"I know I need to talk to her, but honestly, I don't feel that I'm ready and that I can do it productively. Plus, this could be a CLM."

He looks at me quizzically, and I realize he may have never heard that acronym. "Oh, CLM stands for career-limiting move."

He chuckles. "Well, not dealing with it could also be a CLM. So let's walk through your NEW framework to see how it would play out with Joanne. Let's start with the examples first, that might make naming it easier."

I reiterate the examples of her outburst and poor body language in the meeting.

He winces a little. "That sounds a bit judgmental. But I think it's to be expected. How would you describe the examples without the heavy load?"

"I guess I would describe it as how she communicated her frustration around the open business discussion in our meeting last week. I can probably also let her know I've interpreted her body language as frustration during that segment in previous meetings."

WHAT ASSUMPTIONS AND JUDGMENTS ARE YOU MAKING ABOUT OTHERS' INTENTIONS?

"That sounds better."

"But I have to tell you, Peter, it isn't just this situation. I've seen and experienced her brooding dissatisfaction and public outbursts before, and it has me and others on edge. We can't continue to work this way. Every time I have to see her, I wonder which Joanne I'll be meeting with. It's either the logical and thoughtful, albeit terse, Joanne or the one who throws elbows and checks you into the boards like a hockey player. I don't mind her directness, it's when it comes across as an attack that it frustrates me. I heard one of the team members say after the meeting that they didn't want to bring something up because they were fearful of how Joanne would react. That's scary."

"Well, as Yogi Berra said, 'When you come to a fork in the road, take it.' It seems you're at a fork and have to decide if you want to continue on the path of living with this or finding a new path forward. I will admit, I haven't found that path yet with Joanne, but I think your framework for addressing these types of challenges might create that new path. Since you have a specific situation to deal with, it seems using that as an opportunity to talk about how you work together might start that process. So given that, how would you name it using your new framework?"

"Well, before we talked about it, I would've dealt with the outburst, but I think you hit the nail on the head. I think it's about how we work together."

"You already have the examples, so what would you say is the 'why' for Joanne?"

"I could say it's affecting how we work together, but I'm not sure if she cares how I feel about our interactions."

He challenges me. "You're making an assumption there, but maybe it's true. Is there another 'why' for Joanne?"

"I think she would be shocked if she knew people weren't giving her timely or accurate information. After all, she is the accuracy queen."

"So if you were to put it all together, what would you say? Just wing it for now. We can talk about how to refine it if need be. For the moment, I'll pretend I'm Joanne."

Just the thought of pretending he's Joanne makes my hands sweat, but I press on. "I guess I would say, 'Joanne, I want to talk with you about how we work together. In last week's meeting, you expressed your frustration in a way that made me feel defensive and caused the rest of the group to shut down. I've seen this happen before, sometimes by what you say, others by what you communicate with your gestures. I think it's impacting others' abilities to speak freely with you and share the accurate information you need. Heck, I find myself holding back at times.'"

"That's a great start. I like how you talked to how you responded and how you felt versus attacking her. Why don't you write that down before you forget what you just said? And don't rush off to have this conversation just yet. Can I suggest you set it aside, and then refine it after you have a chance to sleep on it? Maybe run it by someone you trust who isn't so close to the situation."

As I finish writing my notes, Peter picks up his coffee and heads out of my office. My first reaction is to drag him back in and help me finish, but I appreciate that this is something I need to think about.

"Let me know what you decide to do and how it goes."

Rather than feeling abandoned, I realize he has confidence in what decisions I make and how I handle this situation. Although still a bit shaky at the thought of having this conversation, I feel clearer and more empowered.

As Peter departs, I'm still thinking I'm missing something. I'm going to deliver this to Joanne, but what happens when I'm done speaking? It feels unfinished. Although in this situation I'm not really asking first, it's an opportunity to ask for her perspective after I tee up this topic. I need to include an invitation for her to share perspective. So I update what I had written with a simple invitation, so it now reads:

> *Joanne, I want to talk with you about how we work togeth-er. In last week's meeting, you expressed your frustration in a way that made me feel defensive and caused the rest of the group to shut down. I've seen this happen before, some-times by what you say, others by what you communicate*

with your gestures. I think it's impacting others' ability to speak freely with you and share the accurate information you need. Heck, I find myself holding back at times. Can you help me understand your perspective and where you think we can go from here?

That last little bit comes to me from my father, who used to say, "Help me understand." When said with true curiosity, it invites others to teach you.

This all looks pretty straightforward on paper, but I know it will be hard in practice. I'm reminded of my high school coach who used to tell us about the Five Ps: Proper Planning Prevents Poor Performance. Hopefully my planning helps to have a better outcome.

I haven't seen him around for a week or so, and Peter is paying one of his early-morning visits to bring me my favorite foo-foo frappuccino from the corner coffee shop. Ya gotta love this guy. It's quiet, and we're probably some of the first souls in the building. The sun is starting to warm my office. As the days are now getting longer, I enjoy soaking in the extra vitamin D everyone needs as we come out of our winter hibernation.

Although we start with some idle chatter, I know why he's here: he's hoping to hear what happened with Joanne. So I oblige. "So, do you want to know what happened as a result of our last conversation?"

He looks eager, like my parents' puppy waiting for his treat. I appreciate his interest.

"First, let me share with you a few things I did after we spoke but before I talked with Joanne." Reflecting on his Yogi Berra quote, I think he knew I wasn't going to take the fork in the road pointing toward continuing to live with this. Although I chose the path of dealing with it, I was so reluctant to have this conversation that at times I was ready to run back down the path so I could take the other fork.

I tell him I really worked to refine the wording. I ran it by a couple of other people outside of the company, including my friend Carl. I had written several versions with a tweak here and a tweak there. The biggest change was adding two things. "First, you asked me about how I contributed, and at first I resisted even thinking about it. Joanne was the one who behaved inappropriately. Then I remembered your quote that it takes two to tango.

"My second excuse for not including my contribution was concern that I'm giving someone ammunition they can use against me. Then my friend Carl suggested that if I did contribute, they're going to bring it up anyway. But he also suggested that although it was a bit vulnerable for me, it showed my willingness to be personally responsible, and it might help others do the same. He said, 'Why would others even consider being vulnerable and taking accountability if others aren't willing to do the same?' That was check and mate for Carl.

"So I added a sentence that said, 'Maybe I'm doing something that's triggering you.' I came to that because it wasn't about the outburst or that segment of the agenda, but how we work together. If I was doing something that triggered her, I would need to deal with that."

I also share with Peter that I had to think about being open to what the other person has to say. That's hard to think about in these situations because what I really want to do is tell them what they did wrong and have them fix it and then get out of there. Thinking about having to sift through

> **HELPING OTHERS BE ACCOUNTABLE REQUIRES US TO ADMIT OUR OWN FAULTS.**

the tension only makes the boulder in my belly grow. "So I added a simple invitation at the end that said, 'I would like to understand your perspective and how we can work together going forward.'"

I point to the IdEA framework poster on my wall and say, "I realize I'm only identifying the topic. There's a whole lot of exploring that's needed before we can even figure out what needs to happen."

"Brilliant," he says. "So how did it go?"

"I'm not done getting ready yet." I smile. "There's more."

I share with him the great advice I had from my brother, not about my opening, but about how to prepare. Rob is a second-degree black belt in karate. He gave me a great mental image to consider using from his martial arts background. He explained that one of the basics is learning the right stance so you can be balanced and keep your center of gravity. He drew the connection to this situation by explaining that I need to make sure I'm balanced. The best thing I can do is make sure I pick a time and place most conducive to both of us. "Find a quiet time, a private place, take some deep breaths, and for god's sake, don't go in all jacked up on caffeine." He said if you're off balance, it's going to be easy to have the conversation degrade, plus it can make the other person feel off balance.

He also explained that my opener is my center. People may want to attack, deflect, or any other host of responses, so I should think about keeping centered on the opener. I tell Peter, "I also realized that if my opener is my center, I need to have that down pat. I could not stammer, stutter, or cloud what I was going to say. So as silly as it may sound, I went through it out loud in my car on the way to work so many times, it kept ringing in my brain as I walked into the office."

Lastly, my brother reminded me of the self-defense classes I took when I was out west. They teach you that when someone comes at you, use their energy to let them pass you by. He said, "If someone goes into attack mode and you're centered, you're more able to let it pass you by. You can do that by listening, and then bring the conversation back to the topic."

"So *now* are you going to finally tell me how it went?" Peter asks with eager anticipation.

"Sure." I pause. "It didn't go well." He looks deflated. "But after thinking about it later, I think that's a good thing. That night when I talked with my brother, he said, 'Look, no one is going to be Gandhi because you think you planned this whole thing out.' He asked me how long I had to prepare for this conversation and how long Joanne had to prepare." It's good to remember that you might be catching the other person off guard, and they deserve the respect of having time to think about it.

I share with Peter the types of things I heard from Joanne and how she responded. First, she turned red, and I could tell she was immediately defensive. Then she said things that in other situations would have either caused me to run for cover or pull out a bigger bully club. She said things like, "The end of this meeting is a waste of time. People just want to sit and complain. There is nothing productive that comes from that part of the agenda. I have far too much on my plate to sit through that BS." There were even jabs at me: "If you can't control your own meeting," "It's your job to keep us on task," and "Why did you include this stupid agenda item?"

"It was hard to sit there and let my hair get blown back, but heeding my brother's advice, I kept centered and didn't respond. I just let her talk. I realized that if I responded, I would only end up in that game of point bludgeoning. I did ask a few questions trying to 'Explore' her perspective, but mostly I just listened.

"I wanted to respond back in kind and tell her, 'If you have a problem, take it up with me privately.' If she didn't like that part of the agenda, then she should have spoken up when we created the new meeting structure. And it wasn't my meeting, it was everyone's meeting. Lastly, I wanted to reprimand her for her childish behavior. I confessed that I wanted to, but I turned that off as responding to my own triggers. Any comment like those would have only escalated the issue, and it wouldn't have helped us resolve this.

"After listening for a while, I came back to the topic I had named in my opening statement, which was about how we work together. I acknowledged her frustration, but said we had to find a better way to deal with these situations, and it wasn't just what happened in our meeting.

"She said, 'Well, I don't know what you want from me.' To which I replied, 'I'm not sure what we need to do,' emphasizing 'we' so it was clear we're in this together, not me against her or vice versa.

"I ended our meeting by suggesting we take a break and come back to it tomorrow after we both had an opportunity to think about it."

"So did you have the follow-up meeting with her?" Peter asks.

"Yeah, but I have to admit, it was preceded by a sleepless night. I spent the evening trying to map out every possible scenario. I would think, 'She'll say this, and I'll say that. Or if she says this, then I'll respond with that.'

"I shared my conversation with Carl as I tried to map out a logic tree of how the conversation would go. He assured me that regardless of how well I planned, I could never account for all possibilities. That my best bet was to get rested, and when we talked the next day, to keep focused on the guardrails. By that, he explained, you need to keep on the topic of how you work together going forward so you can figure out what to do together.

"The next day, for all my planning, the conversation didn't even come close to any of the scenarios I considered. When I arrived at her office, it looked like she might have had a bit of a sleepless night. Because I'm the more talkative of us two, I opened with, 'I appreciate your willingness to talk through this together. I truly want to find a way we can work together that works for both of us. I'm sorry if I caught you off guard yesterday, and I admit I'm a bit hesitant to have this conversation today.'

"I think my honesty helped her drop her guard a bit. She admitted that she knows she has some sharp edges and that it can be off putting. Also, she said she tends to react too quickly and has a bad poker face. If something's bothering her, people know just from her expression. 'Believe me,' she said, 'I've heard that feedback before. It's just hard for me to control.'

"I was impressed she was that forthright, but again, she is always pretty forthright. I've grown to appreciate that about her when we're dealing with business issues. So I told her so. Then I turned back to how we work together in situations like the previous week's meeting, where forthrightness became enflamed and shut people down.

"We had a long conversation, but something this significant doesn't get resolved in one sitting. Even so, I think we both learned something and have some actions to take. Joanne, for her part, agreed to talk to the team and let them know she's aware of how she can come across and that she'll be working on finding better ways to communicate when she gets triggered. For my part, I learned that she thinks I need to be more directive with the team. I actually agreed with her. She's right—there are times when I can lean in more, take control, or keep things on track.

"We agreed that we're both at a critical juncture in the organization and need to make sure we work well together. So to keep the lines of communication open and get these topics on the table before the flames lick at our heels, we agreed to meet once a week, just to check in. No formal agenda, just review the weekly meetings and how we're working together.

"I can see that I can benefit from learning some of Joanne's forthrightness in my leadership style. She also said she's working on her style with her coach. I was shocked when she asked me to give her feedback on how she's doing. I agreed, as long as I could get her feedback on how I'm leading, less on my heels and leaning in more.

"Look, I don't think we solved world hunger by any stretch, but I'm pleased we've started talking on a different level. I also think it's had an impact on the team. Mostly, it has boosted my confidence in dealing with these types of conflict."

Peter says, "Obviously this is confidential, so I don't plan to repeat what you shared. I do think there's something to be learned that can benefit the organization. Also, I think you're ready to loop back with Gayle and the executive team. What do you think?"

"I think I need a little time to put this all together, but I can be ready in a week if you agree."

"I'll get you on the agenda, then. Let's walk through it together if it helps you prepare."

"Absolutely, I'll take the help." So we agree to meet a couple of days before touching base with the executive team.

Chapter 10

Putting It All Together

Game day is upon me, and I'm presenting to Gayle and her staff of seven executives. The challenge was putting it all together in a way that makes sense. It was hard to distill everything I've learned thus far along with the contributions of everyone on the team as well as those who helped me outside of the team, like Peter, Carolyn, Carl, my brother, my father, and so many others. I'm nervous, of course, but my preparation with Peter helped me build confidence.

I start my presentation with a question. "How many of us here are facing some kind of conflict?" Several hands snap right up, a couple rise slowly, cautiously, and a couple aren't raised yet because they don't know if this is a setup.

I follow up by saying, "I'm not here to make us feel uncomfortable about the conflict we face, but to see that we're surrounded by conflict in many different forms. For me, it started in our weekly review meeting, which was rife with conflict, and more importantly, conflict that wasn't being addressed, eroding the foundation of our team and, quite honestly, the organization. For example, how we handle special requests. That was the beachhead where we started as a team trying to find a better way to handle conflict."

I lead into the slide that has the definition of conflict and explain that we found we needed a new way to think about conflict. If we agree we're surrounded by it and can change how we think about it, we might change how we deal with it.

"Defining conflict as a gap captured some attention and created healthy discussion. Some admitted they saw conflict as only those situations where it was a knock-down, drag-out affair. The group came to believe that seeing conflict as a gap might allow us to address situations long before they escalated.

"Also, seeing it as a gap between what we expect and what we experience allows us to depersonalize the situation and possibly have a more productive conversation. We tend to want to make it personal and blame people instead of diving into the situation and what caused it." That point gets some humble nods. "We came up with a few tools to help us see and name the gaps more effectively. I will share those shortly."

I focus on the middle of our definition and the need to create understanding, to see things from all perspectives. Gayle's head of marketing jumps in and affirms the point. "It reminds me of the quote from a philosopher, David Hume: 'Truth springs from argument amongst friends.'"

I nod in agreement. "One of our biggest challenges was making sure we looked at challenges from different perspectives. Even if people don't directly disagree, they have perspectives that can help us. I'm going to share with you a method we created to ask better questions and get really curious."

I shifted then to the last part of the definition: to create better results. "At the end of the day, we need to align around decisions we make as a team. Before, we used consensus and voting with a majority-rules approach. The problem was that those who weren't in agreement might feel left out, or worse, actively go against an agreed to decision. We found that by looking at things from all perspectives, it was easier for someone to align with a decision, even if they didn't agree. By asking, listening, and exploring, people fulfilled one need we all have, and that is a need to be . . ."

Peter jumps in to finish the sentence. "Heard. I've watched this group, and something happens when people are heard and acknowledged. The likelihood that the group will make a decision and stick to it is much higher." He nods in my direction, passing the conversational baton back to me.

Gayle challenges me, politely. "Angela, I'm still struggling with your statement that we're always in conflict. That makes me think we're always at battle stations ready to go to war. That can be stressful for the person and the organization. Can you share more of your thinking around this?"

I smile and take a breath. "I struggle with the same thing. I wish I could come up with a better word than conflict, because people's reaction to the word can elicit the need to dive for cover.

"What I'm starting to see is that conflict falls on a spectrum. On one end is how we traditionally see conflict: eyes bulging, veins popping. What I'm trying to do for myself is see the subtler ways I might be in conflict before it escalates out of control.

"For example, I was having a challenge with one of my supervisors around some simple ways I wanted information to be presented. I would talk with him about it, but I would still have issues with his reports. They weren't major issues, more like annoyances. Previously, I might have let it go, dropped hints, approached it indirectly, or just fixed it myself. What I realized is that by doing that, I might escalate over time as this little gnawing grew. By addressing the conflict when its intensity is lower, I might avoid the heavier-handed approach.

"That's why we built a few tools to help these conversations regardless of where they fall on the spectrum."

Gayle's expression says I answered her question and it's okay to move on.

In my process of preparing for this meeting, I noticed that the IdEA framework fits perfectly with our new conflict definition, like pieces of a puzzle. So that's how I present it.

The IdEA Conversational Framework

Id	**IdENTIFY**	*A gap between what we expect and what we experience . . .*
E	**EXPLORE**	*That leads to deeper understanding . . .*
A	ACT	*And better results.*

I walk through the importance of identifying, exploring, and creating action as represented by our mnemonic, IdEA. From the looks on everyone's faces, I think the simplicity is appreciated.

Gayle's VP of finance says, "It seems this can be used to develop the skills needed to deal with conflict without trying to create a system. If our teams—and quite honestly, those of us here in the room—can get better at identifying and exploring, I think we'll be able to make better decisions faster."

I give a short intro to Identify and explain that we developed a couple of tools to help people name situations that could be creating conflict. "It isn't just about problems that are a conflict, but situations that create conflict. For example, I might be ready to make a decision in customer service, but without others knowing and sharing their perspectives, I could step on a landmine in manufacturing that I hadn't thought of. In that way, I can manage conflict long before I create a larger problem."

I explain that we worked as a team to identify how to explore better, and came up with five types of questions we can use to get better understanding. I give a quick overview of the Five Ws, Why, Risk, Internal Reflection, and Business Impact.

Gayle's VP of finance jumps in again. "So are you recommending that people go through these one by one in order?"

"Actually, no. What we have found is that these help us think about the types of questions we need to be asking. The group jumps around because the answer to one kind of question might lead to a question in another category. Trying to follow this as a rote method can be too constraining. Besides, not every topic lends itself to every possible question in every category. So for lack of a better term, we let the exploration flow."

He seems to like that answer, so I move on to Act. "One of the challenges we had as a team is clearly defining action. There were several problems. First, we didn't leave time to do that when we were discussing a topic, so people would walk out of a meeting not knowing what was agreed to. But more importantly, we didn't convert our understanding into the best action. So we have much more deliberate conversations about what we're agreeing to, what steps we're going to take, and how we're going to follow up. One of the most significant results of our conversation about action is getting clear about what we have control over and impacting what we can control."

That captures Gayle attention: "Tell me more about that."

"Sure, let's use an example. There could be a situation where we might need more resources to complete a project, but we know there's a hiring freeze and we don't have control over it. So would you all agree we might feel we have no control?"

Everyone nods, and I continue. "But finding places where we might have control helps us focus our efforts. For example, are there creative ways to solve the resource constraint, can we negotiate requirements to relieve the constraint, or is there are better way for us to beg for an additional resource from you all?"

The group chuckles, and the VP of finance jumps in. "Like having a clear business case and ROI."

"Exactly," I say. "So overall, this approach was created to help us engage in better conversations on a full spectrum. I would even suggest this approach is what we can use in a majority of our conversations."

I have a slide that outlines the different types of conversations we have in our day-to-day work, like problem solving, team meetings, requirements planning, scheduling, expectation setting, one-on-one coaching, feedback, confrontation, and more.

I share how I've been using this approach in my one-on-one meetings like my weekly reviews with my direct supervisors. My team has become much more effective at coming to meetings prepared to identify the most important things they're working on.

"I find myself continually trying to either identify or help others identify topics, exploring better, and gaining clarity in action regardless of the topic or whether it's one on one or in a team setting. Last month, we hired a new customer service specialist for our team, and I used this approach with her to better understand her expectations and perspectives. We even talked about a couple of things that could become challenges for her down the road. I, for my part, got a much better perspective on the on-boarding process for our team."

Going back to the Identify part of our IdEA framework, I suggest that there are two different angles to identifying topics: either I am identifying, or others are. I start with how we can help others identify.

"I have found that in my one-on-one conversations, I can create immediate focus and get to core issues by asking simple questions that invite the other person to open up. My favorite is, 'What's the most important thing you want to talk about?'"

Gayle's VP of manufacturing says, "Can you repeat that?" as she writes furiously.

As I repeat it, I explain the two parts of that question. "First, 'most important' gets us past the fluffy and unimportant things. But I mention 'you' specifically. I realized I used to spend all this time preparing for my one-on-ones, and quite honestly, we never got to real issues. It was more like a grammar-school teacher grading homework. By shifting to the other person, we got to what was truly important to them, which was a much more engaging topic.

"These types of questions can also help in meetings. I've started my staff meeting with a general question like that, but I've also asked similar, but more specific, questions that open the door to deeper conversations. For example, last week I started our meeting with, 'What is the most important thing we can be talking about that will have a significant impact on our customer response time?' So instead of staff meetings turning into updates and death by PowerPoint, we are talking about real issues. One way we've started opening our meetings is with this question: 'What is the most significant challenge or opportunity you're facing right now?' This is really powerful because it connects the group; it can highlight overlap or commonality and set the context for the meeting. Last week, one of those challenges became the main focus of our meeting.

"I see you've been using the Topic-Briefing Template in your meetings. This is a way to help people identify important topics and get them going. As you may have found, the team, myself included, is getting better at succinctly naming a topic, determining whether it's a challenge or an opportunity, identifying the most important information, and deciding what we want from the conversation."

Gayle pipes in. "I've noticed it, and we've used it too. Do you require people to prepare something before the meeting?"

"Some people come to meetings with the template filled out; some even email it in advance. But we don't limit it to that. Sometimes a topic will come up that we need to address in the moment. The person who raises it might make some notes on the fly, or even use the template as a guide as they talk extemporaneously."

Gayle asks, "So is this what you use when you have to raise a difficult topic with others?"

"Yes and no. I find this approach helps me to name a topic, provide background, and be clear about what I'm asking for. So in that way, it can work both one on one and in a team setting. However, I found the approach needs a little different tactic when giving feedback."

OUR GOAL IS TO HELP OTHERS SELF-ASSESS.

I give an overview of the NEW tool as a way to start the conversation to provide feedback. I see lots of positive body language and conversation about this tool. Clearly this was something Gayle wanted me to address and that the group found to be important. I give them a few examples of how to frame feedback using this tool, and I get more positive response.

The VP of administration asks, "So you take this and go deliver it to people when you need to give feedback?"

"I hate to give a two-handed answer—'on one hand, yes, and on the other hand, no'"—I smile—"but I have found it depends.

"In our day-to-day feedback, I think it's better to help the other person self-assess."

The VP of manufacturing jumps in again. "Can you repeat that?" Again, she is furiously writing. I can see I've hit a chord with the rest of the group.

"Someone much wiser than me said we think our role is to inflict our feedback on others, and that can be rather presumptuous. It assumes we have the whole picture, we know what they need to do, and they need our help to do it. This person suggested that we might need to ask first. To see if they can accurately self-assess and, hopefully, be able to do it in the future when we aren't there."

Gayle jokes, "Like with our children."

The VP of finance says, "And like our children, we aren't always going to be there."

I walk through the feedback loop and the importance of asking first. To let the other person identify. Then if they don't, we can use our NEW framework to name the feedback.

"The other problem with feedback is that we think it's about what they did wrong." I explain the thinking around first helping the other person see what went well, because we easily default to what went wrong. "Also, we need to make sure positive feedback is specific. If we do it right, hopefully the person can continue to repeat those things they're doing well." The executive team likes that we can use the same NEW framework for both positive and constructive feedback, and that we can use the feedback loop as a way to use the IdEA framework to better Identify, Explore, and Act on feedback.

Gayle asks, "What if we have to give them direct feedback on a serious issue? Do we use the same process and framework?"

"This is the other side of the yes-and-no answer I gave before. It would be disingenuous to ask someone how things went if we have to address a serious issue; it can come across like a setup. But we can still use the NEW framework to make sure we identify it properly."

I share that I had a problem with a peer, not naming Joanne, where I used this as a way to tee up a serious issue we needed to address. I shared that I found it was important to really take my time to prepare and even explained what I had learned about being centered. Of course, everyone wanted to know how it went. I think a couple of people might have heard the reverberation from when Joanne blew up.

"I think my biggest takeaway was that it started a conversation, but it didn't solve it. By getting it out on the table, we were able to talk about what happened and come up with things we can do in the future."

I notice I'm getting to the end of my time on the agenda and I should start to wrap up. I didn't get to cover all of what I learned and what we created, but I think I conveyed the essence.

By way of summary, I say, "I think my biggest lessons from challenging myself to deal with conflict are that conflict exists in many forms across a spectrum, that being able to frame topics is a critical skill, and that asking questions helps to create better understanding and better results. At the end of the day, this all comes down to our ability to use the one tool we all have: our ability to engage in productive conversation. I would even been so bold as to suggest that our ability to engineer conversations is our universal leadership tool. The tools and concepts we came up with are here to help us with that."

I don't get a standing ovation. I would be silly to assume that would happen. But the thank-you from Gayle and the rest of the group says it all. Peter is glowing with a look of paternal satisfaction. He walks me out of the boardroom, pats me on the back, and says, "Great delivery. You stuck the landing."

Epilogue

It's been a few months since the executive presentation. The team has really come along, and I no longer feel the soul-sucking drain I experienced when I first joined the company. My position has been elevated from manager to director, recognition of my work and results. I find myself looking forward to work most days, and although I like to be the first into the office and put in a longer day, I am no longer there late at night, and very rarely on weekends.

I continue my morning coffee clutches with Peter, and he continues to treat. Since I'm not burning the midnight oil, I haven't been seeing Carolyn as much at the office. But, we have become friends, and weekends find us hiking together talking about work and life. She has become like my extra sister.

Carl and I continue to chat by phone, and he's been in the area several times over the past months, allowing us to grab a lunch or dinner. I still had the sense he was going to ask me something, yet it was never forthcoming until a week ago when he was in town. Two and two now add up.

Gayle had called an all-hands meeting to announce that our company was being acquired by the same parent company that owned my previous employer. Carl and I were going to be working for the same company again. His trips into town were all part of the due diligence. Over dinner, he shares with me that although we don't compete and we work in related but separate industries, we're definitely going to have opportunities to collaborate. Now I know why I kept sensing a subtext to our conversations.

A couple of months later, I have the privilege of putting three important people in my life in the same place at the same time. I'm taking Peter, Carolyn, and Carl out for dinner as a thank-you. It gives me an opportunity to thank them for their impact on me. I tell each of them what they did and how they contributed to my growth.

As a thank-you, I have given them each a gift: a hand-blown glass globe with a special design embedded inside, an infinity loop. I explain that the loop represents our conversations and the work we did together. "I have had time to reflect on what all of this means to us, and I've come to the conclusion that conversation is an infinite loop. There is really no beginning or end. We're always somewhere in a loop of conversations that precede our involvement and will continue long after our spoken word. Thank you for being part of my loop and for sharing yours."

As we adjourn for the night, I'm warmed by the friendship. I realize that had there not been any conflict when I accepted this position, I would have never had the chance to bond with all three of them, and I wouldn't have had a chance to grow as much as I have the past few months.

Now it's time for me to go tackle more conflicts.

The End

∞

The following pages provide the tools covered in the book. They are provided here in summary form for quick reference, and in some cases additional details are included to aid in application of the tools.

Thriving in Conflict *Definition*

CONFLICT: A GAP BETWEEN WHAT WE <u>EXPECT</u> AND WHAT WE <u>EXPERIENCE</u> THAT LEADS TO DEEPER <u>UNDERSTANDING</u> AND BETTER <u>RESULTS</u>.

The Conflict Spectrum

Although not represented in this fashion, the chart below illustrates that conflict happens on a spectrum. Intensity grows as the impact and frequency increase. By addressing conflict on the lower end of the spectrum, more significant conflicts can be mitigated.

The Conflict Spectrum

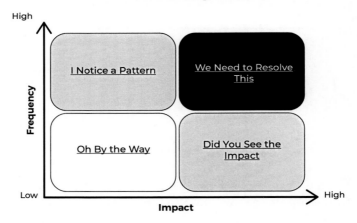

The lower left-hand quadrant, "Oh by the way," is an opportunity to provide observational feedback. By doing so, we can intervene before a pattern or a significant impact emerges. For example, letting someone know they made a mistake as soon as you notice it.

"I noticed a pattern" addresses what happens as the frequency increases. Patterns start to emerge, resulting in greater intensity. This is an opportunity to identify and address a pattern. An example might be repetitive errors in work products or repeated tardiness to meetings.

The lower right-hand quadrant represents those situations where something happens and the impact is significant enough that it requires intervention. In these cases, "Oh by the way" feedback is not sufficient. An example is when someone violates a safety procedure or says something that is wholly inappropriate, a violation of policy, or illegal.

The upper right-hand quadrant is where we tend to focus when we think about conflict: when something has a significant impact and happens on multiple occasions. By seeing the other scenarios that lead us to these situations (i.e. observational feedback), we can reduce the number of times we end up in these high-intensity situations.

The feedback and conversational tools provided in this book are intended to provide productive ways to deal with those situations that occur in any of these scenarios. The method or framework can apply across the spectrum, though the preparation and context will probably change.

Principles of Engagement

In the book, Angela and the team develop principles of engagement as a guide for how they engage each other and to hopefully reduce the amount of conflict. The following is a summary of the principles and a brief description of each. Most of the principles are referenced in the book, but there are some additional ones included here. Use them with your team. An even better approach is to come up with your own principles in your own words that will increase your engagement and manage conflict.

Ask First, Listen Second, Speak Last	As we get older, we lose our curiosity and ask fewer questions. This principle is a reminder to ask more questions *and* to listen. When we have done that, people are more likely to hear what we have to say.
Play Good Politics	We look at politics as a bad thing, when in actuality, we are political animals. There are good politics and bad politics. Good politics requires strong influence skills.
Manage the Drama	There is always drama. Any good movie or book has drama. We need to find ways to create drama that leads the organization forward and minimize drama that holds us back.
Leverage My Gut against Biases	Our gut can be a powerful guide. Inspect what yours is telling you. At the same time, we all have biases. We need to leverage our biases against our gut.

Speak My Truth	There is an old saying: "Speak truth to power." The flaw in that logic is that you have the truth and the only truth. We need to both speak our truth and recognize other truths. Also, it gives permission to everyone to speak their truth.
BLUF	BLUF stands for Bottom Line Up Front. A key skill for any professional is the ability to frame a topic succinctly. BLUF is a reminder to succinctly frame a topic whether one on one or in teams, and even in our written communications.
Manage My Impact	Everyone leaves an impact on their job. Sometimes it's positive, but there are times a positive impact is overused and, as a result, becomes negative. Also, we all have blind spots. We need to consistently seek feedback to see our unintended impact.
Socialize the Messages	We consistently hear that we need to communicate more. This creates more memos, emails, and presentations. Although important, socializing the message is a reminder to communicate but build in a healthy dose of interactions and questions.
Increase Your CQ	CQ stands for curiosity quotient, or the ratio of questions to statements. In conversations, we can seek to increase the number of questions we ask versus what we tell others.
Be a Control Freak	This doesn't mean we have to control everything. It means we can focus on where we have control. This can be empowering, as opposed focusing on things we can't control.

The IdEA Conversational Model

The IdEA Model provides a simple framework to guide any conversation, whether one on one or in a team environment. It illustrates that conversations have three basic parts: identifying, exploring, or acting. Thus the mnemonic IdEA as a simple way to remember the framework. Rather than a script, this can provide a vehicle for anyone to improve his or her conversation skill by becoming more skilled at identifying what is being discussed, exploring more thoroughly, or defining action.

The IdEA Conversational Framework

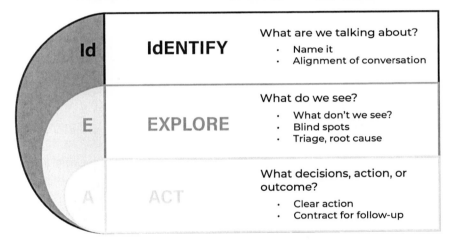

Id	**IdENTIFY**	What are we talking about? · Name it · Alignment of conversation
E	EXPLORE	What do we see? · What don't we see? · Blind spots · Triage, root cause
A	ACT	What decisions, action, or outcome? · Clear action · Contract for follow-up

Identify

Breaking down the framework, the following shows that when we identify a topic, we can either help someone else identify what they want to discuss, or on the other side of the coin, do a better job of more succinctly identifying the topic we want to discuss. For example, the Topic-Briefing Template provides a way to tee up a topic, and the NEW framework is a simple way to introduce feedback. The feedback loop method provides a simple way to help others more accurately self-assess.

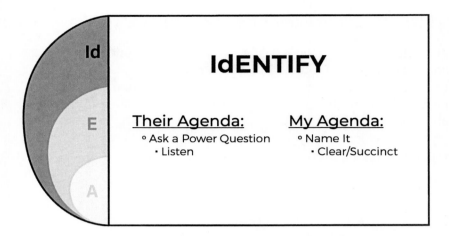

Explore

Exploration is the center or the engine of any conversation. Most people admit it's important to ask more questions; however, knowing what to ask can be challenging. The Explore loop below provides some of the types of questions to ask. The Five Ws—who, what, when, where, and how—are good data questions and can help to gain a new perspective on a situation.

"Why" is treated separately because it's a different type of question. "Why" helps us understand the meaning or purpose someone has related to a topic. By understanding someone's "why" or purpose, we are helping to drive motivation and, ultimately, change. For example, why a topic is important to them or how they want to show up in a given situation. We are surrounded by risks, so it's important to identify what's at risk. This, too, like the "why" questions, can help with motivation and driving change.

Some simple risk questions include "What are you most afraid of?" or "What can happen if this isn't addressed?"

We all have a tendency externalize, to look outside of ourselves. The internal reflection is intended to help us look at ourselves, how we might have contributed to a situation, and even how we feel about a situation.

Lastly, if we're having a conversation about something, it's because it's impacting our business and what we do. In planning for an outcome, we can be better prepared if we can identify how it is impacting the business, like cash, revenue, costs, employee satisfaction, customer experience, etc.

Exploring: Level 2 – Deeper Understanding

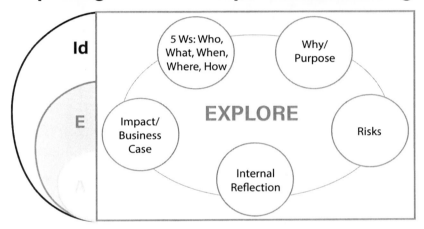

Act

Many times, the challenges and opportunities we face don't get resolved because we fail to adequately define the solution or action. Like the old saying "The road to hell is paved with good intentions," we start with the best of intentions, but often fail in execution. We can increase the likelihood of a better outcome if we do three things when discussing action. First, we need to have a clearer picture of the outcome. Using our Five Ws again (who, what, when, where, and how), we can paint a more vivid image of the action we're defining. For example, asking how they want to approach it, when they want it to be completed, what milestones are important, what it will look like, etc. The more we define the outcome, the more likely we are to complete it.

Sometimes, our plans are so all-encompassing as to be over-whelming, freezing us in our tracks. We can move things forward by asking, "What is the most powerful step I can take right now?" The key word "powerful" helps us see we have power, "you" focuses on what the individual can do, and "right now" injects immediacy. Another key concept in defining action is focusing on where we have control. It's easy to point out the innumerable things we can't control, like the economy, management, other groups, and customers. Focusing on where we have control is empowering.

Lastly, we can improve the likelihood of a result by being clear about the next steps and how to follow up, and ensuring we plan for the likely barriers we will encounter. Too often we assign due dates instead of asking the other person when and how they want to follow up.

Creating Action

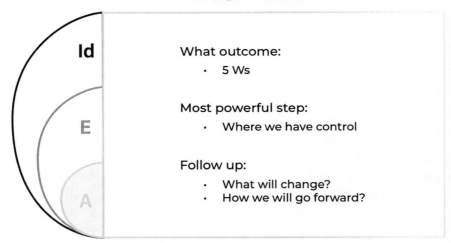

Id

What outcome:
- 5 Ws

Most powerful step:
- Where we have control

E

Follow up:
- What will change?
- How we will go forward?

A

Preparing to Deliver Feedback

Many times we offer feedback before we have clearly defined what was seen, heard, or experienced. Sometimes it's obvious, but as intensity increases, it becomes more likely we need to stop, reflect, and gain some clarity.

The questions below provide examples of what to consider when thinking about and preparing to deliver feedback, whether it's observational feedback or high-intensity confrontation. The questions are not intended as a questionnaire or audit, nor as questions to ask in sequence. By asking ourselves these types of questions, and yes, even asking others, we can get better clarity, manage our emotions, and provide better feedback.

- ✓ What have I seen, heard, and experienced? Identify examples objectively and without judgment or assumptions.
- ✓ Why is it bothering me?
- ✓ What is this about for me?
- ✓ Why would this be important for the other person to resolve?
- ✓ What assumptions or judgments am I making about this person or situation?
- ✓ How might others explain this situation in a more objective way?
- ✓ Is this a problem or just a symptom?

The Topic-Briefing Template

The Topic-Briefing Template (TBT) provides a simple outline to frame a topic. Although in the book it is used in a meeting, it can be used anytime to help outline a topic in a way that is clear and succinct. Keeping it to one page will help to create focus. Like the translated quote of French mathematician Blaise Pascal, "If I had more time, I would have written a shorter letter." It takes time to be succinct. This template is intended to aid in that effort.

Topic-Briefing Template

TOPIC NAME	
Name the topic, issue, opportunity, or challenge in two sentences or less.	
BACKGROUND	
Share *most important* background: ✓ Who, what, when, where, how ✓ Control: Where we/I have control, what we/I can control, what we/I can't control ✓ What has led to this being a topic that needs to be discussed ✓ Why is this important/What is the compelling reason? ✓ Barriers and enablers to resolving ✓ Risks ✓ Strategic implications ✓ Customer impact/considerations ✓ Other stakeholders ✓ Any actions already taken, being taken, or being considered ✓ Timing considerations ✓ Financial considerations (cash, revenue, cost, profit, investments, ROI) ✓ Ways we/I may have contributed ✓ Ideal outcome/Your best guess of what to do	
OUTCOME—"THE ASK"	
What can we realistically accomplish from this discussion? ✓ Decision/approval/validation ✓ Flush out/define the topic/issue ✓ Understand root cause ✓ Identify important questions ✓ Identify risks ✓ Identify resources ✓ Create an initial plan	

The outline includes some suggested considerations. Naming the topic (the top box) is important. Too many times someone starts describing a topic, but does not name it effectively. The middle box is for identifying the most important and relevant facts, not all of them. It is likely the background will need to be trimmed down. "The Ask" is to ensure clarity around what is desired from the conversation. Whether one on one or in a team setting, treat the topic box (the topic) and the bottom box (the ask) as the guardrails for the conversation. Ultimately, the Topic-Briefing Template provides a simple way to organize talking points before introducing an important topic.

Facilitating a Meeting
Using the Topic-Briefing Template

The following provides an outline to use when employing the TBT and the IdEA Model to engage in better, more focused, and more results-oriented conversations in team meetings. It's recommended that teeing up the topic be limited to five minutes or less. Allow the discussion leader uninterrupted time to cover the topic, background, and the ask.

The exploration process is, by design, a messy process. Participants will want to jump in. Encourage participants to ask questions first, and use the top box (topic) and bottom box (the ask) as guardrails if the conversation goes off track. There is no script to this, since each situation is different. Using strong facilitation techniques can help to build understanding.

Often meetings fail because there is no clearly defined action. It takes about fifteen minutes to wrap up a topic. Before time runs out, ask a closing question. A closing question is a variant of "the ask," like what risks do you see, what resources should we pursue, or what decision would you make. Asking people to write down the answer versus just spouting them out provides time to consider a response. Asking each person to share what they wrote helps to ensure you hear from everyone. Again, there is a variety of facilitation techniques that can help this process, far too many to cover in the space allowed here.

1. IDENTIFY: *The Five-Minute Brief*
   a. Use the Topic-*Briefing* Template (5 min.).
   b. To keep focus, have one discussion leader.
   c. This can be done on the fly, if it has not been prepared in advance, by asking someone to use the TBT to organize his/her thoughts as they share a topic.

2. EXPLORE: *Deeper Understanding*
   a. Use the Explore questions from the IdEA Model.
   b. Use this as an opportunity for everyone to build questioning skills.
   c. Recommend the group start with questions before jumping in with ideas.
   d. Ensure balanced participation from all participants.

3. ACT: *What Are We Committing To?*
   a. It takes fifteen minutes to wrap up a topic.
   b. Use the "A" in the IdEA Model.
   c. Make sure to hear from everyone.
   d. Close by sharing what's going to happen from the conversation, even if the only action is going back to think it through more thoroughly as a result of the feedback.

Delivering Feedback Using the NEW Framework

Very few people have been trained on how to deliver feedback. As a result, it can come across in ways that do not provide better understanding or better results. NEW represents the three things that effective feedback needs regardless of whether it's lower-intensity observational feedback or higher-intensity confrontation:

Name It: Name the feedback objectively and specifically. Calling someone lazy or disrespectful is not effective, but naming it as being late with deliverables or communicating in a particular way helps to name it more effectively. If you aren't sure how to "name it," start with the next part (examples) since considering what you see and experience can point to the topic and gain clarity.

Example(s): Clearly stating the examples ensures that the other-person understands exactly what you're referring to. For example, "You were late" might not be specific enough, but stating, "You were late last Friday by an hour" ensures you are talking about the same thing. If it's something you observed in passing, it might only require one example. As frequency increases, you will need to share the specifics that illustrate a pattern. If it's something that has happened numerous times, you don't need to name every situation, but provide enough examples to demonstrate the pattern.

Why: It's important to state why addressing this feedback is important *to them*. Sure, we can tell them why it might impact you, the company, or others. However, they may not care, but they will darn sure care about how it might impact them. Some examples include the person's bonus, how they are perceived, others' willingness to support them, a performance review, raises, and yes, even the person's employment with the company. If there is a "why" for the other person, it's more likely something will change.

When we think of feedback, we tend to think only of constructive or corrective feedback. We may not be thinking of positive feedback. Also, how we deliver accolades may not be the best method. We pat people on the back and say, "Good job." That isn't feedback, it's cheerleading. Of course, it's important to cheerlead, as it creates excitement and energy. What it might not do is ensure that the other person repeats the thing they have done well. Why?

Because they may not know specifically what they did well or why it's important.

Providing positive feedback can follow the NEW framework and help to clearly name the feedback, share specifics of what was done well, and drive motivation by identifying why it's important for them.

Of course, there are subtleties to how, when, and where to deliver positive and constructive feedback that are not covered here, but this simple framework provides a way to prepare feedback in a better way.

Building Robust Feedback Loops

Even though the NEW framework is intended to help deliver more effective feedback, there is more to the process. There are some fundamental flaws we can encounter when we deliver feedback, including expecting the other person to be open to feedback, believing we know what happened to require the feedback, and assuming it's our job to inflict feedback on someone else.

Instead of thinking we need to follow up and give feedback, wouldn't it be great if we helped others to more accurately self-assess how they're doing and ultimately self-correct? Of course, there are still times we need to deliver timely feedback, and we can augment that by applying one of the principles of engagement: "Ask first, listen second, speak last." If we want to build robust feedback loops, start by asking others how it went before we share our feedback. The feedback loop below is intended to provide an overview of how this can work for individuals and teams.

First, start by asking how something went, like a meeting, a presentation, or a work product. Rather than asking a general question, ask first, "What went well?" This is important because most people will focus on what went wrong. Focusing on what went well is important since it increases the likelihood the person saw it themselves and is more likely to repeat it.

It can also help you, because you may not have noticed what went well. You are also less likely to see the positives when you have significant constructive feedback to provide. As the diagram shows, make sure you explore what the other person says, since it helps gain clarity. Once you have explored the positives, if there's something you think they did well and he/she didn't name it, use the NEW framework to share what you noticed.

After you've covered the left side of the loop, now you can switch to the right. Think about the question you ask. The right side is labeled EBI, which stands for Even Better If. This is more encompassing than asking for problems or what went wrong. Of course you will hear those kinds of things, but you might also hear things that could make something even better. Just like the positives, make sure you explore what happened. For example, someone might share they had errors in the report. However, by exploring it, you might find out they didn't get the data until midnight the day it was due, or that they're not good at catching errors.

By exploring, you get clarity and will have a greater likelihood of finding a good resolution. If there is an area of improvement or EBI the other person didn't notice, now you can introduce your feedback using the NEW framework. Again, once you introduce your feedback, take the opportunity to explore what the other person might have experienced, but be mindful you could have misunderstood.

You might wonder, "Wait, I prepared this feedback and the other person named it, so I never got to use it. Did I waste my time?" The short answer is no. First, you are ready *if* you need to deliver feedback. Also, the more opportunities you have to prepare feedback, the better you will get at doing it in the future. Also, remember the Five Ps: Proper Preparation Prevents Poor Performance. You are dealing with someone's identity and an important topic. It's worthy of taking an opportunity to prepare even if you don't have to use it.

Once you've gone through the loop, now you're ready to use the Act skills from the IdEA Model to determine next steps and action. Make sure you are clear about what's going to happen as a result of the conversation.

The feedback loop is just one way to start building a robust culture of feedback.

The Self-Assessment Feedback Loop

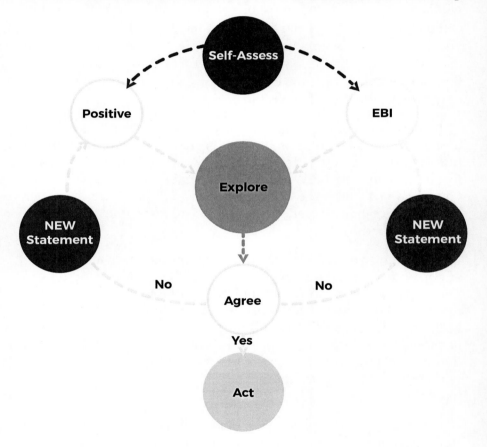

About the Author

Doug Johnston has spent his career seeking ways to engineer better, more impactful conversations for himself and others. This is central to his work whether delivering workshops, speaking at conferences, facilitating leadership forums, advising clients on special projects, or leading strategic planning events.

After enjoying a successful executive career in a Fortune 100 corporation as well as various midsized companies, Doug founded his consultancy, Impact4Results, in 2002. He has worked with over ten thousand professionals in a variety of industries at all organizational levels, from the executive suite to front-line employees. Over the years, Doug developed conversational tools designed to engage in more effective conversations for both one-on-one and team settings, whether it's to provide feedback, manage expectations, develop professionally, or address any of the other myriad topics we all encounter. Testimonials to his effectiveness rave about his ability to engage a broad range of audiences, his business knowledge, expertise in leadership, and overall facilitation skills.

Doug has two adult children and lives in Rochester, New York, with his wife of over thirty years. His hobbies include cycling, traveling with his wife, and reading on a variety of topics.

Other Books by Doug Johnston

Exponential Leadership: Formulating YOUR Impact

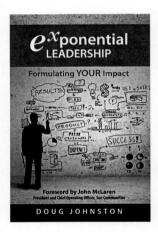

Exponential Leadership is a business novel—it follows the journey of a senior leader as he learns that leadership can be considered from an analytical or a quantitative perspective. Many senior leaders consider leadership to be something amorphous; here we learn that by gradually building a strong, workable formula we can apply this process to our everyday business lives to generate powerful, impactful results within our organizations.

A common theme across all of Doug Johnston's work is *converting the focus of our thinking from short-term results to long-term impact*. This book is a heart string in his personal journey to attain such lasting impact for himself and spread the same message to others.